casseroles and pies

CONTE

Beef with Guinness, page 13.

Pork Vindaloo, page 47.

Bacon, Herb and Vegetable Pie, page 53.

Sweet Vegetable Curry, page 83.

Lamb Stew with Rosemary Dumplings, page 35.

The Publisher thanks the following for their assistance in the photography for this book:
Villeroy & Boch; Redlemans Fabrics; Belvedere Gallery; Janet Niven Antiques; Studio Haus; all Sydney.

Chicken and Sugar Snap Pea Parcels, page 75.

Seafood Stew, page 103.

Herbed Fish Tartlets, page 97.

The test kitchen where our recipes are double-tested by our team of home economists to achieve a high standard of success and delicious results every time.

When we test our recipes, we rate them for ease of preparation. The following cookery ratings are on the recipes in this book, making them easy to use and understand.

A single Cooking with Confidence symbol indicates a recipe that is simple and generally quick to make – perfect for beginners.

Two symbols indicate the need for just a little more care and a little more time.

Three symbols indicate special dishes that need more investment in time, care and patience—but the results are worth it.

Inside front cover: Quick Pork Casserole, page 51.

Casserole & Pie Basics

Casseroles are delicious, simple to make and nutritious. Meat, chicken, seafood as well as vegetables and pulses are all suitable for this method of cooking. Pies are a wonderful treat for guests and family alike. This guide to the fundamentals will help you feel confident with both styles of cookery.

Casseroles

There is a lot of confusion about what a casserole consists of. The word is French and means *stew*. We often interpret the word to mean the actual pot or baking dish, with a tight fitting lid, in which the food is cooked. We also think of it as the food baked in such a dish. However, the important aspect of a casserole is the process of long, slow cooking which results in a tender, flavoursome dish. Whether this is achieved in an oven or on top of a stove doesn't matter – it is still a casserole.

Hearty Shepherds' Pie is a great family favourite, page 36.

Casserole cookery has many advantages over other methods of cooking. Perhaps most important is that it is generally better to use the more economical cuts of meat, which helps with the budget. As well as this, it is usually cooked and served in the same dish, which means less washing-up.

Most casseroles and curries will improve in flavour if cooked in advance and refrigerated overnight or even for a couple of days. The same dish can be used for cooking, refrigerating, reheating and serving. When ready to use, remove from the refrigerator and skim off any fat that has formed on top. This will make the casserole a much healthier meal. When reheating, the food should be brought to the boil and then simmered slowly for approximately 20 minutes. Casseroles may be reheated in the microwave on a medium-high setting.

Any leftover casserole portions can be used as pie fillings. They may need thickening with a little blended cornflour and water.

Casseroles can be varied by using toppings such as pastry, scone dough, mashed potato or pumpkin.

Following a few simple rules will ensure that you feel happy with casserole cookery.

For a successful result, it is important to seal in the juices of pieces of meat or poultry by first browning quickly over a fairly high heat. Do this in batches, turning frequently and setting aside each batch until it is all done. If the pan is too crowded, the meat will stew and become tough. Sometimes the meat is tossed in seasoned flour before browning. This helps to add flavour as well as thicken the liquid in the cooking process.

Below you will find some helpful hints to use when cooking the recipes in this book.

Meats

For casserole cookery, the cheaper cuts of meat are generally the best choice, not only for economy, but for increased flavour.

For a beef casserole, cuts such as blade, chuck, round or topside steak are ideal. They generally have more flavour than expensive cuts like fillet or rump.

The same applies to cuts of veal such as veal shanks which have an excellent flavour and texture.

For lamb casseroles, cuts which we don't often make use of produce very tasty meals. For example, neck chops and lamb shanks lend themselves to this type of cookery and are very easy on the budget.

Pork fillets and other cuts of pork which are suitable for casseroling have recently been made much more accessible to the home cook. They are reasonably priced, quite lean and full of flavour.

Unlike the expensive cuts, which are usually cooked quickly, the cheaper cuts of meat are best when slowly simmered in liquid in a casserole dish. This process tenderises the meat and produces a delicious meal. The fibres of cheaper cuts, while initially becoming tough, break down while cooking and become succulent. You can tell when the meat is cooked because the pieces will easily break up with a fork.

Poultry and Game

Chicken, turkey, rabbit and duck are all suitable for casseroling. They become very tender and add variety to the dinner table. Even when larger old birds are used they are transformed into a tasty, tender meal. Make sure the food is simmered gently, not boiled, otherwise the meat will toughen.

Whole chicken, chicken pieces, thighs, drumsticks and wings are readily available from chicken shops and some butchers. They can all be used for a casserole. Rabbit is available from some butchers. You will find duck and turkey in some chicken shops and shops that specialise in game. In the freezer section of supermarkets you will find turkey in pieces (like turkey breast roll), which are convenient to use.

Seafood

Seafood is high in protein and offers a wide variety of flavours and textures with the use of different types of fish, crustaceans and molluscs. Seafood is easy to prepare and does not take quite as long to cook as meat and poultry. The secret of a moist fish casserole is to ensure it is not overcooked and the cooking temperature is low. Otherwise, it will become tough and dry. For casseroles, the sauce is often prepared first and fish added later.

Vegetables

Vegetables are highly nutritious and make an economical meal. Some vegetable dishes are more suitable for serving on the side with a main course or as a first course. Slow-cooking vegetables like potatoes, parsnips, turnips, or sweet potatoes are an ideal addition to meat and poultry casseroles. Not only do they add flavour but will help thicken the sauce, thus eliminating the need for any flour or thickening agent. The faster cooking vegetables such as snow peas, broccoli or mushrooms are usually added towards the end of cooking time to prevent them becoming too soft.

Legumes and pulses are high in protein and fibre and add variety to your cooking. Some need overnight soaking to make them soft and cut down cooking time. If you are in a hurry, place the pulses in a saucepan, cover well with hot water and bring to the boil. Simmer for a couple of minutes, skimming froth from the top. Remove from heat and allow to soak for approximately one hour. After draining, they will be ready for use.

Casserole Dishes

When choosing a casserole dish, buy one that can be taken straight from freezer to oven or microwave. A tight-fitting lid is essential to ensure moisture is retained. The size of the dish is important. If it's too small, the liquid might overflow. If it's too large, the food will dry out because the liquid will reduce too quickly. The food should come approximately three-quarters of the way up the dish for the best result.

If the dish becomes stained during cooking it is best to allow it to cool and then soak it overnight in cold water. This will make most stains easy to remove.

Cutting of Vegetables and Herbs

When slicing vegetables, try to keep the pieces uniform in size. Some recipes are best with chunky vegetables, some with finely sliced ones which will merge into the sauce.

There's a trick to chopping fresh herbs. Use a large sharp knife and place one hand on the handle, the other hand on the top of the blade. Hold the top of the blade in one place, chop with the other hand in a swivelling motion to finely cut herbs. It's a very quick and efficient method.

When slicing cucumbers for a sweet and sour sauce, first cut them in half and then scoop out the seeds. Cut the flesh, into julienne strips, the same as other vegetables to be used.

Tinned tomatoes will often remain whole even after prolonged cooking. You can strain them and place the tomatoes on a board for chopping, but it is messy and inefficient. A simpler way is to roughly chop the tomatoes with a pair of kitchen scissors, while they are still in the tin.

Trimming Meat

While cheaper cuts of meat are often well marbled with fat, any large pieces of fat and sinew should be removed. Neither of these will break down in the cooking process and it's a most unpleasant sensation to find a piece of fat or gristle in your mouth.

You will need a sharp knife to trim fat and sinew from meat.

Cut the meat into even-sized cubes. The size of the cubes depends on the type of meat and on the dish but somewhere between 2–3 cm is the most usual. If the cubes are too small, the meat will fall apart into shreds during cooking and the dish will not look appetising.

Cut meat into pieces approximately the same size for best results.

Coating Meat

If you coat the meat cubes in flour seasoned with salt, pepper and often herbs and cook them on all sides in oil or butter, a crusty brown coating will form on the meat, giving it an attractive appearance and a delicious taste. Coating with flour will also help to thicken the casserole – usually once flour has been used to coat meat you don't need any other thickener.

There are two ways of coating meat in flour. Whichever method you use, try to avoid doing it too far ahead of cooking time, or the flour will be absorbed by the moisture in the meat. It will no longer be a coating and in fact will change the whole texture of the dish. If for some reason the flour is absorbed, re-coat the meat just before use and shake off any excess.

The first method is to place plain flour on a sheet of greaseproof paper and mix in a little pepper and salt. Using your hands or tongs, turn meat cubes in flour, coating on all sides. Shake off excess flour.

Toss all sides of cubes in seasoned flour on a sheet of greaseproof paper.

The second method is to put flour and seasonings into a plastic bag, add meat cubes – not too many at a time – and shake until thoroughly coated. Remove from bag. Shake off excess flour.

In plastic bag or freezer bag, place seasoned flour. Toss meat in batches.

Casseroles and the Freezer

Casseroles will store well in the freezer for up to three months. Food should be frozen as soon as it has cooled. Skim any fat from the surface of the cooled casserole before freezing.

Freezer bags or plastic bags are the easiest to use because of the irregular shapes of food. An ideal method is to place the bag inside a cake tin or other rigid container of suitable size and shape. Spoon the casserole into the bag, tie loosely and put the tin or container in the freezer. When food is hard, remove bag from tin, squeeze out as much air as possible and seal securely with a twist tie or adhesive tape. Label and date before returning to the freezer until required.

Of course, if you have cooked a large quantity, you may not wish to freeze the whole lot together. In this case, freeze in smaller bags in the portions required for future use.

It is best to thaw casseroles completely before reheating but if you are in a hurry it is possible to reheat straight from the freezer. Remove from bag or container and heat either slowly in a saucepan on top of the stove or in a casserole dish in the oven. To avoid cracking the dish, place in a cold oven and heat to 220°C. Heat for about 30 minutes depending on the amount of food. If you are cooking dumplings or a pastry top, do not add until the casserole is warm.

Spoon cooled casserole into bag which has been placed inside tin.

When food is hard, remove bag from tin, squeeze air out, tie.

When to boil and when to simmer

As a general rule in casserole making, the ingredients are browned, liquid is added, the food is brought to the boil, the heat is reduced and then it is covered and simmered slowly until tender.

A dish is boiling when large bubbles appear in quick succession on the surface. Never boil a casserole for prolonged periods, otherwise the meat will become tough and stringy and any vegetables will break up and look unattractive.

Simmering is when tiny bubbles appear – at a slower pace – on the surface of the food. If there is too much liquid, uncover and simmer until liquid has reduced.

When liquid is boiling, big bubbles appear on surface in rapid succession.

Casseroles are slowly simmered. Tiny bubbles will appear on the surface.

The Essence of Flavourings

When flavouring casseroles with herbs, it's important to be able to remove the herbs when the dish is ready to serve. A piece of very wilted parsley or a well cooked bay leaf is not a pleasant surprise to the taste buds (and is difficult to remove with any grace).

Herb & celery bundles
Tie a bunch of fresh herbs and a small piece of celery together with a piece of string. When added to a casserole it will add a lovely flavour and is easy to remove before serving.

Clove-studded onion
Peel an onion and press cloves into it. Add to casserole for flavour. Remove before serving. Cloves are usually difficult to remove when the meal is ready to serve and this makes the task easy.

Bouquet garni
Place a mixture of fresh herbs such as parsley, lemon thyme and a bay leaf on a square of muslin, tie into a bundle with string. The herbs will add flavour and can be easily removed.

Importance of Browning

When browning pieces of meat, fish, chicken or vegetables, oil is usually a better medium than butter, because butter burns at a comparatively low temperature. However some dishes use a mixture – oil prevents butter from burning and butter adds a nutty flavour. Brown all sides. The idea is to seal in the juices and give a coating, not to cook the food.

Brown meat quickly on all sides, over high heat, to seal in juices.

Turn chicken frequently when browning to prevent sticking.

About Stock

A well-prepared stock is the foundation of most casseroles. Beef, veal and chicken are excellent to use and, fortunately, the cheaper cuts of meat like chuck steak have the most flavour.

The butcher will chop any bones into suitably sized pieces. These should first be browned in a little oil in the oven.

Place browned bones in a large deep pan. Cover well with water, add flavourings such as onion, celery, carrot, whole peppercorns and a bouquet garni made of a bay leaf, sprigs of thyme and parsley. Garlic may also be used sparingly. Too much may overpower the subtle stock flavour.

Simmer stock gently, uncovered, for up to 2 hours, being careful not to boil.

If making chicken stock, the back and neck can be used or the whole bird simmered, the liquid kept and the meat used separately.

Fish stock is easy to make using fish trimmings and is described on page 104 in the Seafood section of this book. It should not be cooked longer than the amount of time given in the recipe because the taste will become bitter.

Leftover fresh stock can be frozen for future use. Freeze in 1-cup quantities in plastic bags. These can be used for making soups or casseroles.

When you don't have time to make your own stock, ready-made stock is now available. Chicken specialty stores sell frozen stock which is very convenient and good to have on hand.

Supermarkets sell a wide variety of stocks, in both dry and liquid form, which can be used instead of freshly made stock. Some commercial stocks are quite salty so if using them, don't add salt to the recipe until you have tasted the food.

Place a little oil in a deep baking dish, add bones, brown both sides in oven.

Place browned bones in large, deep pan, add water and other ingredients.

Pies

Nothing compares with the wonderful aroma of a pie baking in the oven. The smell of pastry and filling blend to evoke pictures of a hearty winter meal.

Pastry is an excellent method of enclosing food to retain its flavour and moisture. The result is a soft, succulent filling which contrasts beautifully with the crispness of the pastry and is very pleasing to the palate.

Savoury pies are always popular and are also very versatile. They can be made in various sizes and shapes and you can use your imagination to decorate the top for impressive presentation. As a main course, for either lunch or dinner, pies will please both adults and children. Some are a nutritious meal in themselves. Others may need the accompaniment of vegetables or salad. Little meat pies are always a hit at children's parties. Some pies are great picnic food. Small pies with fillings like curried meat and vegetables or spinach in cheese sauce, often made with filo pastry, make an excellent first course.

As you will see from the recipes in this book, most meats and poultry, as well as seafood and vegetables, adapt well to pie cookery. Pies can be frozen successfully as long as the filling is suitable for freezing and the pastry has not already been frozen. For best results, a frozen pie should be reheated in a slow oven.

All that is necessary to become a successful pie maker is a good pastry and a variety of fillings. You can make pies seem different each time you make them with the addition of suitable herbs and spices to either the pastry mix or the filling.

All about Pastry

Pastry, like pies, is very versatile. Not only can it be used for making pies but it will add variety to your winter cookery when added as a topping to oven-cooked casseroles. Pastry can be made in a larger quantity than required and frozen for future use.

Pastry for savoury pies is made by combining flour, salt, shortening and liquid and sometimes egg or egg yolk. The quantity of each ingredient varies

Steak, Onion & Tomato Pies, page 29.

depending on the type of pastry being made and the texture that is required for a particular recipe. The addition of herbs or other flavourings is optional and depends on personal taste and the filling being used.

Types of Pastry

There are three main types of pastry used for pies – shortcrust, puff and filo. There are many variations of these. Shortcrust is very simple to make and suitable for both savoury and sweet pies. Puff pastries are a little more difficult. They are quite rich and give a nice flaky texture. Rough puff pastry is similar to puff but easier to make and not as rich. It can be used as an alternative to puff in

most recipes that call for puff pastry. Filo pastry is paper-thin and is generally purchased rather than made at home. Another simple pastry is suet crust which can be used for dumplings or as the top of a casserole.

Ready-rolled short or puff pastry can be purchased from the supermarket and these save considerable time.

Basic Shortcrust Pastry: Shortcrust pastry is so named because it has a short (i.e. crunchy) texture and will break easily. If you are making it by hand, it is best if your hands are cold so, if necessary, before you begin hold them briefly under cold water. The butter and liquid should also be cold. To make pastry for a two-crust 23 cm pie shell, sift 2 cups of plain flour and 1 teaspoon salt into a bowl. Chop 125 g unsalted butter into small pieces and add to the flour. Using your fingertips, rub the butter into the flour, lifting as you do it. When it resembles fine breadcrumbs, gradually sprinkle in 4–5 tablespoons of cold water gently mixing with a knife or fingers until the mixture comes together. Form into a ball. Wrap in plastic wrap and refrigerate for 20 minutes. When ready to use, divide into two, place half on a floured board, and flatten with your hand. Roll pastry away from you using short strokes, working quickly and rotating the dough until it is about 3–4 cm bigger than the container you will be using. Roll around rolling pin and lift into greased tin or dish.

If you want a rich shortcrust, increase butter to 160 g and when mixture is fine and crumbly, add 1–2 beaten egg yolks and mix in quickly, adding a little water only if necessary.

Pastry Secrets

The secret of a light and crisp pastry is to make sure the dough is not overworked. Whether the mixing is done by hand or with a food processor, as long as you do it quickly, it will be easy to handle and roll.

The amount of liquid required for pastry varies depending on the texture of the flour so the liquid must be added gradually in small amounts until the mixture comes together. It should then be formed into a ball, wrapped and refrigerated for 15–30 minutes. Remove and roll on floured surface to required size. Pastry should always be cooked in a preheated oven, never one that has not yet reached the temperature specified in the recipe.

Chicken and Sugar Snap Pea Parcels, page 75.

If you are using a food processor for making pastry, measure the flour and salt into the bowl. Chop unsalted, cold butter into even-sized pieces. Add the butter to flour. If you have a pulse button on your processor, use it to process the mixture briefly. If not, turn the machine on for short bursts, checking texture constantly.

When making pastry by hand, make sure ingredients and your hands are cold. If necessary, run your hands under cold water. Dry your hands. Place flour and salt into a bowl. Chop unsalted butter into even-sized pieces and add to flour. Rub pieces of butter into flour using your fingertips. If you prefer, use a knife in a cutting motion.

When using commercial pastry, place required amount on lightly floured surface and roll out with floured rolling pin, always rolling in the direction away from your body.

Measure flour into processor bowl, add chopped butter, process briefly.

When rubbing butter into flour, use only your fingertips, not palms.

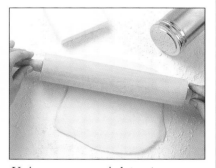

Using commercial pastry saves time. Roll out on floured surface.

Process until fine and crumbly being careful not to overprocess.

Work quickly and gently, rubbing in butter until it resembles breadcrumbs.

With a pastry brush, cover each sheet of filo with melted butter.

If using a food processor to make pastry, it is important not to overprocess the mixture. Otherwise, the pastry will become tough and hard to handle. When flour and butter mixture is fine and crumbly, liquid can be added, a few drops at a time until mixture starts to come together. Stop processing action as soon as this happens. Pastry is ready for use.

Rub the butter into flour until it resembles breadcrumbs. Depending on the amount of butter in a recipe, the mixture may resemble fine powdery breadcrumbs or, if a higher proportion of butter is used, coarse, fresh breadcrumbs. At this stage, you can mix in the liquid, a little at a time, until you feel the mixture start to bind together. Gather together and roll into a ball.

When a recipe calls for filo pastry, it is important to take care in handling the fine, delicate sheets. Lay the pile of pastry sheets out flat and cover with a wet tea-towel to prevent drying out. Using a pastry brush, brush one sheet at a time with melted butter placing sheets on top of each other as you go. Wrap unused sheets in foil, store in refrigerator.

Decorationg Pies

Traditionally, savoury pies were decorated whereas sweet pies were left plain. This was done so that guests could differentiate when a selecton of pies was presented on the sideboard.

Nowadays, you can let your imagination run wild. There are many ways to decorate pie tops to make them appealing. Some of these are shown below.

Little children will be delighted if you put their initials on individual pies or put shapes which they will recognise on big pies.

You can make pastry roses or daisies, leaves or even small pastry sculptures such as a boat or a cricket bat if you want to commemorate a special event.

Personal decorations such as these are one of the joys of home-made pies. Your family and guests will love this special personal touch.

Add colour to the top of savoury pies by arranging thin slices of vegetable on the filling before covering with pastry. Use a fluted cutter to make a hole in the centre of pastry before placing over filling. Vegetable will show through. Use tomatoes, capsicum or other vegetables.

Chicken and Ham Pie, page 70.

It is important to brush pastry with beaten egg or a little milk before baking. This will ensure a rich, deep colour and an attractive shine when pastry is cooked.

Sesame seeds or ground nuts may be sprinkled over before baking.

Using a sharp knife and a ruler will help with this decoration.

Bacon, Herb and Vegetable Pie, page 53.

Place on top of pie and let strips fall casually down in an attractive shape.

To decorate top of pie, roll out pastry trimmings and cut a rectangle about 20–30 cm long x 10 cm wide. Leaving a 2 cm uncut section along one edge, cut 5 mm strips with a sharp knife. Brush with beaten egg white. Roll up and place on top of pie. The strips will fall down to form an attractive top.

THE FINISHING TOUCHES

Roll out pastry trimmings and with a small circular cutter, cut circles and fold them in half, then fold over again and place each one around edge of pie top. Brush with beaten egg.

To give pie edge a higher puffed finish, cut a long strip of pastry, nick all along one side with a knife. Place pastry strip around rim of pie dish on top of pastry base. Brush with beaten egg.

Roll out pastry trimmings, cut leaf shapes to place around edge of pie, overlapping each one. For a more realistic effect, use a sharp knife to mark veins on leaves. Brush with beaten egg.

Make a lattice top. Cut sheets of puff pastry into long strips 1.5 cm wide. Interweave strips to form a lattice pattern. Lift pastry, place over top of pie overhanging the dish. Trim edges.

Place pastry in tin to come 2 cm above top of tin. Trim pastry and roll inwards down towards pie top. Brush with beaten egg. Make indents with finger around edge of pie to form fluted pattern.

With a decorative cutter, make shapes all over pastry sheet, reserve cut-outs. Place pastry on top of pie. Place cut-outs between holes. Fork around edges, trim. Brush all over with beaten egg.

Baking Blind

Baking blind will ensure that the base pastry is crisp even if the filling is a moist one. If you don't do this, you may find the pastry base is soggy.

First, preheat oven to hot 220°C (425°F/Gas Mark 7). Roll out pastry large enough to cover base and sides of greased tin leaving about 2 cm overhanging (to allow for shrinkage). Ease pastry loosely into tin. Place tin on a tray, cover and refrigerate for about 20 minutes.

When ready to bake, remove from refrigerator and trim pastry edge. Cut a sheet of greaseproof paper large enough to cover pastry-lined tin. Line pastry shell with the paper and spread a layer of dried beans or rice evenly over paper. Bake for 10–15 minutes, remove from oven and discard paper and beans. Return tin to oven and cook pastry for a further 5–10 minutes.

Before filling with pastry, brush tin all over with melted butter or oil.

Place pastry in tin overhanging sides. Cover, refrigerate on tray.

Fill paper lining with rice or beans before baking in preheated oven.

After baking, remove from oven, discard paper and rice or beans.

BEEF & VEAL

BEEF WITH GUINNESS

Preparation time: 20 minutes
Total cooking time: 1 hour 45 minutes
Serves 4–6

1 kg round steak
30 g butter
1 tablespoon olive oil
2 large onions, chopped
2 tablespoons plain flour
1 cup Guinness
1 cup beef stock
3 large carrots, peeled and cut
   into 3 cm pieces
2 large parsnips, peeled and cut
   into 3 cm pieces
2 bay leaves
$1/2$ cup chopped fresh parsley

➤ PREHEAT OVEN to warm 160°C (315°F/Gas Mark 2–3). Trim meat of fat and sinew. Cut into 3 cm cubes.
1 Heat butter and oil in a large frying pan; add cubes of meat in small batches and cook for 4–5 minutes or until browned on all sides. Remove meat from the pan with slotted spoon or tongs and place in a casserole dish.
2 Add onions to pan and cook gently 3–4 minutes or until brown. Add flour and stir over low heat 2 minutes or until flour is lightly golden.

3 Add combined Guinness and stock gradually to pan, stirring until mixture is smooth. Stir constantly over medium heat for 2 minutes or until mixture boils and thickens; boil for another minute. Place carrots, parsnips and bay leaves in the casserole dish. Pour sauce over. Cover and cook for $1^1/2$ hours or until meat and vegetables are tender. Sprinkle parsley on top just before serving.

COOK'S FILE

Storage time: Recipe may be made up to three days ahead. Store, covered, in refrigerator. May be frozen.
Variations: Replace round steak with chuck steak. A boned leg of lamb, cut into 3 cm cubes, may be used as a substitute for beef steak. Half a cup of prunes, halved and pitted, can be added during the final 30 minutes of cooking. The prunes will add sweetness to the recipe.
Hints: Serve with mashed potatoes or boiled new potatoes and steamed beans or broccoli.
Guinness is a traditional Irish draught stout. It has a strong, bitter taste and is dark in colour. When added to beef dishes, it gives the meat a very distinctive taste. You may find the taste of Guinness too strong. If this is the case, a lighter ale may be used as a substitute in this recipe.

VEAL AND MUSHROOM CASSEROLE

Preparation time: 20 minutes
Total cooking time: 2 hours
Serves 4

750 g veal steaks
1/4 cup plain flour
30 g butter
1 clove garlic, crushed
1 tablespoon Dijon mustard
1 cup cream
1/2 cup white wine
1 tablespoon chopped fresh thyme
1 cup chicken stock
375 g button mushrooms, halved

➤ TRIM MEAT of excess fat and sinew. Cut in 1 cm strips.
1 Toss meat with flour in plastic bag, shake off excess flour. Heat butter and garlic in heavy-based pan. Add meat and cook quickly in small batches over medium heat until well browned. Drain on paper towels.
2 Return meat to pan. Add mustard, cream, wine, thyme and stock. Bring mixture to boil, reduce heat. Simmer, covered, 1 1/2 hours stirring occasionally.
3 Add mushrooms; cook for a further 15 minutes or until meat is tender. May be served with pasta and julienned, steamed vegetables.

COOK'S FILE

Storage time: This recipe may be made one day ahead and kept in an airtight container in the refrigerator. Reheat gently.
Hint: Seeded mustard or hot English mustard may be used instead of the Dijon mustard.

OSSO BUCCO

Preparation time: 20 minutes
Total cooking time: 2 hours
Serves 4–6

2 tablespoons plain flour
freshly ground pepper
6 osso bucco (veal shanks,
    cut into 4 cm pieces)
2 tablespoons oil
2 cloves garlic, crushed
1 large onion, chopped
2/3 cup dry white wine
2/3 cup beef stock
425 g can tomatoes
1/4 cup tomato paste
1/2 teaspoon caster sugar

Gremolata
1/3 cup fresh parsley sprigs
1 clove garlic, crushed
2 teaspoons grated lemon rind

➤ PREHEAT OVEN to moderate 180°C (350°F/Gas Mark 4). Lightly grease a 12-cup capacity baking dish with oil or melted butter. Combine flour and pepper on a sheet of baking paper. Toss osso bucco lightly in seasoned flour; shake off excess.

1 Heat oil in heavy-based pan. Cook meat quickly on both sides over medium-high heat until well browned; drain on paper towels. Transfer meat to casserole dish.

2 Add garlic and onion to pan. Cook, stirring, until onion is just soft. Add wine, beef stock, undrained crushed tomatoes, paste and sugar. Bring to boil; reduce heat and simmer for 5 minutes.

3 Spoon sauce over meat. Cover dish with foil and bake 1³/₄ hours or until meat is tender.

4 To make Gremolata: Finely chop parsley. Combine parsley, garlic and rind in bowl. Just before serving, sprinkle Gremolata over Osso Bucco.

COOK'S FILE

Storage time: This dish may be cooked up to one day ahead and stored, covered, in refrigerator. Reheat when required. Before serving, prepare Gremolata and sprinkle over Osso Bucco. Freeze up to one month.

Note: Osso Bucco is a traditional Italian dish made from veal shanks that are cut into thick circular pieces. The marrow in the bone adds flavour to the recipe. Osso Bucco is usually served with Risotto Milanese, which is a creamy rice dish flavoured with stock and wine.

APRICOT VEAL BIRDS

Preparation time: 30 minutes
Total cooking time: 30 minutes
Serves 4–6

8 (100 g each) thin veal steaks
1 cup cooked rice
125 g finely chopped dried
  apricots
1 tablespoon finely chopped
  glace ginger
1/4 cup chopped fresh coriander
2 tablespoons oil
30 g butter

Sauce
1 onion, sliced in rings
1 cup apricot nectar
1/2 cup good quality white wine
1/4 cup French onion soup mix

➤ PREHEAT OVEN to warm 160°C
(315°F/Gas Mark 2–3). Trim meat of
any excess fat and sinew.
1 Using a meat mallet or rolling pin,
flatten steaks, between plastic wrap,
to an even thickness.
2 Combine rice, apricots, ginger and
coriander in small bowl, mix well.
Place steaks on a flat surface. Place
spoonful of filling along one end of
each steak; roll and tie up securely
with string at regular intervals.
3 Heat oil and butter in heavy-based
pan. Cook meat quickly in single
layer over medium-high heat until
well browned; drain on paper towels.
Arrange rolls in casserole dish.
4 To make Sauce: Remove excess
oil and butter from pan, leaving about
1 teaspoon. Add onion and cook for
2–3 minutes over medium heat until
well browned. Add combined apricot
nectar, wine and soup mix. Stir over
low heat until mixture boils and
thickens. Remove from heat and pour
over rolls. Cover, bake for 25 minutes
or until meat is cooked through and
tender. Remove string from rolls
before serving. May be served with
salad greens or steamed vegetables.

COOK'S FILE

Storage time: This dish is best
eaten on day of making.
Variation: Thin slices of beef steak
can replace veal. Use chopped dried
fruit medley instead of dried apricots.

BEEF GOULASH

Preparation time: 20 minutes
Total cooking time: 2 hours
15 minutes
Serves 4

1 kg chuck steak
2 tablespoons oil
2 large onions, sliced
2 cloves garlic, crushed
6 teaspoons ground sweet
paprika
1 tablespoon plain flour

¹/₄ cup tomato purée
1 cup red wine
1¹/₂ cups beef stock

➤ TRIM MEAT of excess fat and
sinew.
1 Cut meat into 2 cm cubes. Heat oil
in heavy-based pan. Add onion and
garlic. Cook over medium heat for
2 minutes or until golden. Add meat
to pan in batches. Cook for 5–10
minutes or until well browned.
Return all meat to pan.
2 Add paprika and flour and cook,
stirring, for 1 minute.

3 Stir in tomato purée, red wine and
stock. Bring mixture to boil, stirring
constantly. Reduce heat, simmer,
covered, 2 hours or until meat is
tender. If desired, a dollop of sour
cream may be stirred into sauce just
before serving. Serve on a bed of
pasta, noodles or steamed rice.

COOK'S FILE

Storage time: This recipe may be
made a day ahead and stored in an
airtight container in the refrigerator.
Variations: Use chicken instead of
beef but reduce the cooking time.

1

2

3

BEEF WITH BEER, ONIONS AND POTATOES

Preparation time: 15 minutes
Total cooking time: 2 hours 15 minutes
Serves 4–6

750 g beef topside
40 g packet French onion soup mix
1 tablespoon plain flour
2 tablespoons oil
12 small pickling onions
2 cloves garlic, crushed
375 ml can (1 1/2 cups) beer
1 cup beef stock
2 medium potatoes, cubed

TRIM MEAT of excess fat and sinew, cut into 2 cm cubes.
1 Combine soup mix and flour in a plastic bag. Toss meat lightly in seasoned flour; shake off excess. Heat oil in heavy-based pan, cook meat in batches over medium-high heat until well browned; drain on paper towels.
2 Add onions and garlic to pan. Cook, stirring, until onions are browned.
3 Return meat to pan with beer and stock; mix well. Cover and simmer over low heat, stirring occasionally, 1 3/4 hours or until beef is tender. Add potatoes, cover, simmer further 5 minutes. Uncover, simmer 15 minutes or until sauce is slightly thickened.

COOK'S FILE

Storage time: This dish can be cooked one day ahead and reheated. Store, covered, in refrigerator. Suitable for freezing.
Hint: Use any type of beer in this recipe. Use two large onions, cut into wedges, in place of pickling onions.

VEAL WITH BABY VEGETABLES

Preparation time: 40 minutes
Total cooking time: 1 hour 35 minutes
Serves 4–6

750 g stewing veal
4 cups cold water
salt and pepper
60 g butter
2 tablespoons plain flour
375 g button mushrooms
18 baby new (cocktail) potatoes
6 baby turnips
12 baby carrots
1 1/2 cups (250 g) fresh or frozen peas
1 cup (250 g) broad beans
1 cup stale breadcrumbs
1 clove garlic, crushed
1/4 cup chopped fresh parsley
1 teaspoon chopped fresh thyme
45 g butter, melted

➤ TRIM MEAT of excess fat and sinew. Cut veal into 2.5 cm cubes.
1 Place veal in large heavy-based pan. Add water, salt and pepper. Cook over low heat for 30 minutes or until veal is partially tender. Remove from heat. Drain liquid, reserving 2 cups.
2 Heat butter in pan, add flour. Cook 1 minute, gradually add reserved liquid, stirring until mixture is smooth. Stir over medium heat 2–3 minutes or until mixture boils and thickens; boil for 1 minute; remove from heat.
3 Preheat oven to moderate 180°C (350°F/Gas Mark 4). Trim mushrooms, potatoes, turnips and carrots. Cut into uniform size pieces. Firmly pack into an 8-cup capacity ovenproof casserole dish. Add peas and beans. Arrange veal pieces over the top; season. Pour sauce over. Cover, bake 45–55 minutes or until vegetables are tender. Combine remaining ingredients and sprinkle over casserole. Bake uncovered for further 15 minutes or until golden and crisp.

COOK'S FILE

Storage time: Make one day ahead.
Hint: If casserole has too much liquid, remove some before adding crumbs.

Beef with Beer, Onions and Potatoes (top) and
Veal with Baby Vegetables.

SWEET AND SOUR MEATBALLS

Preparation time: 20 minutes
Total cooking time: 1 hour 20 minutes
Serves 4–6

1 large cucumber
1 large carrot
1 red capsicum
1 kg lean beef mince
1 cup fresh white breadcrumbs
1 egg, lightly beaten
1 tablespoon Worcestershire
  sauce
1 tablespoon chilli sauce
1 tablespoon chopped fresh
  parsley
2 tablespoons oil

Sauce
2 tablespoons soft brown sugar
$1/3$ cup white vinegar
2 tablespoons barbecue sauce
2 tablespoons tomato sauce
2 cups pineapple juice
1 tablespoon cornflour
2 tablespoons cold water
440 g can pineapple pieces,
  drained

➤ PREHEAT OVEN to warm 160°C (315°F/Gas Mark 2–3). Halve cucumber lengthways, then widthways.
1 Scoop out seeds. Cut into thin matchstick strips. Cut carrot into 5 cm-long matchstick thin strips. Cut capsicum into thin strips. Combine beef, breadcrumbs, egg, sauces and parsley in a large bowl. Use hands to mix well. Roll 2 teaspoonsful of mixture into balls.
2 Heat oil in heavy-based pan. Cook meatballs in small batches over medium heat for 3 minutes or until well browned, drain on paper towels.
3 To make Sauce: Place sugar,

vinegar, sauces and juice in medium pan. Cook over medium heat until sugar has completely dissolved. Bring to boil. Remove from heat. Blend cornflour with water in small jug until smooth. Add to pan, stir over medium heat for 3 minutes or until sauce boils and thickens. Place meatballs, cucumber, carrot, capsicum and pineapple in casserole dish. Pour Sauce over top. Bake for 1 hour. Serve with rice.

COOK'S FILE

Storage time: Meatballs may be made in advance and frozen. Defrost, reheat gently, prepare sauce.
Hint: For a fast and easy sweet and sour sauce, use the bottled variety available in supermarkets.
Use a sweet chilli sauce if you prefer a milder flavour.
Variation: Chicken or pork mince may be used instead of beef. Reduce the cooking time slightly.

1

2

3

VEAL SHANKS WITH CREAM AND THYME

Preparation time: 20 minutes
Total cooking time: 2 hours 30 minutes
Serves 4–6

2.5 kg veal shanks, cut into
    4 cm pieces (osso bucco-style)
2 bacon rashers (150 g)
2 large onions
1 large carrot
1 tablespoon olive oil
1/2 cup plain flour
1 teaspoon garlic pepper
1/4 cup olive oil, extra
2 cups good quality white wine
1 cup chicken stock
2 tablespoons chopped fresh
    thyme
2 cloves garlic, crushed
1 teaspoon cornflour
1 cup cream
1 cup peas

➤ TRIM MEAT of excess fat and sinew. Cut bacon into 2 cm pieces. Cut onions in thick slices. Cut carrot into 1 cm pieces.

1 Heat oil in large heavy-based pan. Add bacon, onions and carrot, cook over medium heat for 15 minutes or until softened. Remove pan from heat and set aside.

2 Combine flour and pepper in a plastic bag. Toss veal lightly in seasoned flour; shake off excess. Heat extra oil in heavy-based frying pan. Cook veal shanks quickly in small batches over medium-high heat until well browned. Place veal shanks on top of bacon mixture.

3 Drain excess oil from frying pan. Add half the wine. Bring to boil, reduce heat, simmer 1 minute. Pour over the veal. Add remaining wine, stock, thyme and garlic. Return pan to stove. Cover and simmer over a low heat 1 1/2 hours or until meat is tender. Stir occasionally.

4 Blend cornflour and cream in a small jug or bowl until smooth. Add to casserole. Bring to boil, boil for 1–2 minutes or until mixture thickens slightly. Add peas, stir until heated through. May be served with potatoes and freshly steamed vegetables.

COOK'S FILE

Storage time: This dish can be made up to two days in advance. Skim off any fat that has formed on the surface. Reheat gently before serving.
Variation: This recipe can be made using oxtail instead of veal shanks.

Hints: Trim 20 spring onions 2 cm from the bulb. Lightly fry in 30 g melted butter until tender. Add to casserole with peas.

Veal shanks are available from the butcher. Ask the butcher to cut them into pieces.

If you don't have time to make your own chicken stock, it is available in cube form or as a liquid that is ready to use straight from the carton. You will find both at supermarkets.

VEAL A L'ORANGE

Preparation time: 20 minutes
Total cooking time: 2 hours 30 minutes
Serves 4

2 kg veal shanks, cut into
   3 cm pieces
1 cup plain flour
salt and pepper
30 g butter
1 tablespoon oil
1/2 cup good quality white wine
2 cups chicken stock
1 cup orange juice
1 tablespoon finely grated
   orange rind

2 medium carrots (250 g), cut
   into matchstick strips
2 medium leeks (350 g), cut
   into matchstick strips
2 medium parsnips (200 g), cut
   into matchstick strips

➤ TRIM VEAL of excess fat and
sinew. Combine flour, salt and pepper
on a sheet of greaseproof paper. Toss
veal shanks lightly in seasoned flour;
shake off excess.

1 Heat butter and oil in a large
heavy-based pan. Brown veal quickly,
in batches, over medium heat for
about 5 minutes. Drain each batch on
paper towels. When all meat has
been browned, return it to pan.

2 Add wine, stock, juice and rind,
bring to boil. Reduce heat, simmer,
covered, for 1 1/2 hours or until tender,
stirring occasionally.
3 Add carrot, leek and parsnip and
cook uncovered for 30 minutes.

COOK'S FILE

Storage time: This recipe may be
made a day ahead. Store, covered, in
refrigerator.
Variation: Half a cup of lemon juice
can be substituted for half of the
orange juice. Lemon or lime zest will
give this recipe a delicious flavour.
Hint: May be served with boiled
rice or pasta and steamed beans,
broccoli or cauliflower.

1

2

3

SPICED BEEF

Preparation time: 20 minutes
Total cooking time: 1 hour 45 minutes
Serves 4–6

1.5 kg piece fresh silverside
1/3 cup soft brown sugar
1 teaspoon ground cinnamon
1 teaspoon ground nutmeg
1 teaspoon ground cardamom
1 teaspoon ground black pepper
1 orange, cut into quarters
1 large onion, cut into quarters
1 cup water
1/4 cup red wine vinegar

➤ PREHEAT OVEN to warm 160°C (315°F/Gas Mark 2–3). Trim meat of excess fat and sinew.

1 Place sugar, cinnamon, nutmeg, cardamom and pepper in small bowl. Mix well to combine. Rub meat all over with sugar mixture, pressing on firmly with fingers. Place meat in a deep casserole dish.

2 Place orange and onion around meat, pour in combined water and vinegar. Cook covered for 1–1 1/2 hours or until meat is tender.

3 Remove meat from dish, cover and set aside. Remove orange pieces from cooking liquid; strain remaining liquid into shallow pan and cook uncovered for 10 minutes or until reduced by half. Meat may be served warm or cold, sliced, accompanied by the sauce.

COOK'S FILE

Storage time: Silverside is excellent served cold. Refrigerate overnight immersed in cooking liquid. When required, slice meat and serve with a crisp green salad.

Hint: A whole piece of rump or topside steak can be used in place of fresh silverside.

This dish used to be traditionally served at Christmas in many places in England. It included juniper berries. The modern versions use different combinations of spices for variety.

1   **2**   **3**

TEXAS PASTIES

Preparation time: 30 minutes
Total cooking time: 1 hour
Makes 10

1 medium (80 g) potato, peeled
1 tablespoon oil
1 onion, sliced
250 g lean beef mince
240 g can kidney beans, rinsed, drained
$1/3$ cup fresh or frozen peas
130 g can creamed corn
$2/3$ cup beef stock
3 teaspoons cornflour
2 tablespoons water
5 sheets ready-rolled shortcrust pastry
1 egg, lightly beaten
paprika, ground

➤ CUT POTATO into 1 cm pieces. Preheat oven to hot 210°C (415°F/ Gas Mark 6–7). Line an oven tray with baking paper.

1 Heat oil in a heavy-based frying pan. Add onion, cook over medium heat until soft. Add mince, cook until well browned, using a fork to break up any lumps.

2 Add potato. Cook, stirring, for 3 minutes. Add kidney beans, peas, corn and stock. Bring to boil; reduce heat and simmer, stirring, 3 minutes. Blend cornflour and water in small bowl until smooth. Add to pan, stir until thickened. Remove from heat; cool to room temperature.

3 Using a 14 cm round cutter, cut 10 circles from pastry sheets. Place $1/4$ cup of prepared filling on centre of each pastry round. Brush edge of pastry rounds with a little water, bring edges together to enclose filling, forming a semi-circle.

4 Pinch sealed edge with fingers. Place on prepared oven tray. Brush pasties with beaten egg, sprinkle with paprika. Bake in preheated oven for 35 minutes or until lightly browned and filling is heated through.

COOK'S FILE

Storage time: Pasties can be made a day ahead and stored, covered, in refrigerator. Pasties may be frozen for up to six weeks and reheated in a moderate oven when required.

SPICY GINGER AND BEEF CURRY

Preparation time: 15 minutes
Total cooking time: 1 hour 45 minutes
Serves 4–6

1 kg blade steak
2 tablespoons vegetable oil
2 cloves garlic, crushed
2 large onions, chopped
2 tablespoons finely grated fresh
  ginger
1 small red chilli, finely
  chopped

salt and pepper to taste
1 teaspoon ground turmeric
1 teaspoon curry paste
1 small eggplant, finely chopped
1 cup coconut milk
3/4 cup beef stock

➤ PREHEAT OVEN to warm 160°C
(315°F/Gas Mark 2–3).
1 Trim meat of excess fat and sinew.
Cut meat evenly into 3 cm cubes.
2 Heat oil in large heavy-based pan.
Add meat in small batches, cook over
medium heat until well browned all
over. Remove from pan, drain on
paper towels. Place in casserole dish.

3 Add garlic, onion, ginger, chilli, salt
and pepper, turmeric and curry paste
to pan. Cook over low heat for
1 minute. Add eggplant, coconut milk
and stock; simmer for 3 minutes.
Carefully pour curry sauce over beef,
cover. Bake for 1 ½ hours or until
beef is tender. Serve with rice.

COOK'S FILE

Storage time: Make curry up to
three days in advance. The flavour
will improve in this time. Store, covered, in refrigerator. May be frozen.
Hint: Use bottled chopped chilli in
place of fresh chilli.

OXTAIL WITH TOMATO AND BLACK BEAN SAUCE

Preparation time: 40 minutes
Total cooking time: 3-4 hours
Serves 4–6

2 oxtails
1/2 cup plain flour
salt and pepper
45 g butter
2 tablespoons oil
2 cloves garlic, finely chopped
1 large onion, finely chopped
1/2 teaspoon ground cumin
3 large ripe tomatoes (750 g),
    peeled and chopped
1/2 cup water
2 tablespoons black bean
    sauce
pinch cayenne pepper

➤ TRIM OXTAIL of excess fat and sinew. Cut into 3 cm pieces. Combine flour, salt and pepper on a sheet of greaseproof paper. Toss oxtail lightly in seasoned flour; shake off excess.

1 Heat half the butter and oil in a large heavy-based pan. Cook oxtail in small batches over medium heat until well browned. Drain on paper towels. Transfer oxtail to an 8-cup capacity ovenproof 'dish.

2 Wipe out pan. Heat remaining butter and oil. Add garlic and onion. Cook over medium heat 5 minutes or until tender. Add cumin, tomatoes and water. Simmer over low heat 10 minutes or until mixture reduces and thickens. Add black bean sauce and cayenne. Mix well.

3 Spoon tomato mixture over oxtail. Cover and bake in preheated warm 160°C (315°F/Gas Mark 2–3) oven for 3–3 1/2 hours or until the oxtail is very tender. Serve with a crisp, green salad or freshly steamed vegetables.

COOK'S FILE

Storage time: Cook three days before required, cover, refrigerate. This will allow the flavours time to develop. Skim fat from the surface. Reheat gently and serve.

Hints: Oxtail is a very popular winter dish. It has plenty of tasty meat and makes a hearty meal. Ask the butcher to cut it up.

Black bean sauce is available from the supermarket.

1

2

3

4

STEAK AND KIDNEY PIE

Preparation time: 40 minutes
Total cooking time: 2 hours +
  20 minutes resting
Serves 6

1 kg chuck or round steak
300 g lamb kidneys
$1/4$ cup plain flour
2 tablespoons oil
2 onions, chopped
$1/2$ cup beef stock
$1/2$ cup good quality
  red wine
1 tablespoon Worcestershire
  sauce
2 teaspoons English mustard
375 g puff pastry
1 egg, lightly beaten

➤ TRIM MEAT of excess fat and
sinew. Cut into 2 cm cubes.
1 Cut kidneys in half, remove fat.
Toss meat and kidneys lightly in flour
and shake off any excess.
2 Heat oil in a large pan. Cook meat
quickly, in small batches, over
medium-high heat until browned; drain
on paper towel. Add onions to pan and
cook 5 minutes until just tender.
3 Return meat to pan with stock,
wine, sauce and mustard; bring to the
boil. Reduce heat. Simmer, covered,
for $1 1/2$ hours, stirring occasionally.
Remove pan from heat and allow to
cool completely.
4 Transfer meat mixture to a 23 cm
5-cup capacity round pie dish. Roll out
pastry to 3 mm thickness. Cut two
long strips to fit lip of pie dish. Brush
lip with egg and press strips of pastry
into place, pressing to seal joins; brush
with egg. Cut a circle of pastry large
enough to cover top of pie. Cut out
decorative shapes with a small fluted
cutter. Place pastry top on pie, pressing lightly onto strip. Brush pie top
with egg. Fork edges, and decorate pie
with pastry shapes. Preheat oven to
hot 210°C (415°F/Gas Mark 6–7).
Place pie in refrigerator for 20 minutes, to prevent pastry from shrinking
while cooking. Remove from refrigerator, bake for 30 minutes, until pastry
is golden. Serve immediately.

COOK'S FILE

Storage time: Leftover pie will
keep for up to two days. Cover and
store in the refrigerator.

BEEF AND PORK WITH RED WINE

Preparation time: 10 minutes
Total cooking time: 2 hours 30 minutes
Serves 4–6

1.2 kg rump steak
400 g pork belly
1/2 cup plain flour
salt and pepper
200 g speck
2 medium onions
1 large carrot
2 tablespoons olive oil
2 cloves garlic, crushed
2 teaspoons finely grated
 orange rind
1 tablespoon chopped fresh
 thyme
2 cups good quality red wine
2 bay leaves
1/2 cup pitted black olives,
 sliced

➤ TRIM MEAT of excess fat and sinew. Cut rump steak and pork belly into 3 cm cubes. Toss lightly in seasoned flour, shake off excess. Cut speck into 1 cm cubes.

1 Cut onion into thick slices. Cut carrot into 1 cm-thick slices. Heat oil in large heavy-based pan. Add speck and cook 3 minutes until brown. Remove from pan. Add rump and pork belly, cook quickly over medium-high heat until well browned. Drain on paper towels. Add onions and carrot, cook over medium heat 15 minutes or until softened. Stir in garlic and orange rind.

2 Return speck, rump and pork belly to pan with carrot and onion mixture. Sprinkle the fresh thyme into pan.

3 Add red wine and bay leaves. Return pan to heat. Bring to boil, reduce heat to low. Simmer covered for 2 hours or until meat is tender. Add olives, stir until heated through. May be served with pasta tossed in extra chopped fresh herbs.

COOK'S FILE

Storage time: This dish can be made up to two days ahead. Store, covered, in refrigerator. Reheat just before serving. May also be frozen in airtight container up to one month.

Variation: Use pork spare ribs in place of pork belly. Cut each rib into three pieces. Use thick bacon rashers in place of speck. Cut into 3 cm pieces. Speck is available from delicatessens and butchers. Replace dried bay leaves with fresh if available.

STEAK, ONION AND TOMATO PIES

Preparation time: 10 minutes
Total cooking time: 2 hours
Makes 4

750 g chuck steak
plain flour
2 tablespoons oil
1 large onion, thinly sliced
1¹/₂ cups beef stock
1 teaspoon soy sauce
2 teaspoons cornflour
1 tablespoon water
2 sheets ready-rolled shortcrust
  pastry
1 tomato, sliced
1 egg, lightly beaten
2 sheets ready-rolled puff
  pastry

➤ TRIM MEAT of excess fat and sinew. Cut meat into 1 cm cubes.

1 Toss meat with flour in plastic bag, shake off excess. Heat oil in heavy-based pan. Cook meat quickly in small batches over medium-high heat until well browned; drain on paper towels.

2 Add onion to pan, cook over medium heat until soft. Return meat to pan. Add stock and soy sauce. Bring to boil; reduce heat. Simmer, covered, 1¹/₄ hours, stirring occasionally, or until tender. Blend cornflour and water in small jug or bowl until smooth; add to pan. Simmer, stir until thickened. Remove from heat and cool slightly.

3 Preheat the oven to hot 210°C (415°F/Gas Mark 6–7). Cut each pastry sheet in half diagonally. Line four 12 cm individual pie tins with shortcrust pastry, trim edges. Place one-quarter of the filling in each pastry case. Top with tomato slices. Brush edges with a little beaten egg, top with puff pastry, seal and trim edges. Cut remaining pastry scraps in leaf shapes. Place on pies. Brush tops with egg, bake 25 minutes or until golden. Remove pies from tins, place on oven tray and bake for a further 5 minutes or until pastry base is cooked through.

COOK'S FILE

Storage time: Pies can be cooked up to two days ahead. Store, covered, in refrigerator. Suitable for freezing.

Hint: If pie tins are unobtainable, foil pie containers are available in some supermarkets.

Variations: Pan-fried mushrooms can be used instead of tomato. Add two teaspoons curry powder to step 2 if making curried meat pies.

1

2   **3**

29

BEEF AND VEGETABLE CASEROLE WITH MUSTARD SCONE TOPPING

Preparation time: 30 minutes
Total cooking time: 2 hours 30 minutes
Serves 4

1 kg chuck steak
1/2 cup plain flour
salt and pepper
1/4 cup oil
2 medium onions, chopped
1/2 cup good quality red wine
425 g can tomatoes
1/2 cup beef stock
1 tablespoon Worcestershire
    sauce
2 tablespoons tomato paste
1 bay leaf
250 g small button mushrooms
200 g broccoli florets

Mustard Scone Topping
2 cups self-raising flour
1/2 teaspoon salt
20 g butter, chopped
1 tablespoon seeded mustard
2 tablespoons chopped fresh
    parsley
3/4 cup milk
1 tablespoon milk, extra

➤ PREHEAT OVEN to moderate 180°C (350°F/Gas Mark 4). Lightly grease an 8-cup capacity casserole dish. Trim meat of fat and sinew. Cut into 3 cm cubes, toss in seasoned flour, shake off excess.
1 Heat half the oil in heavy-based pan. Cook meat quickly in batches over medium-high heat until well browned. Drain on paper towels.
2 Heat remaining oil in large heavy-based pan. Add onion, cook over medium heat until soft. Remove from heat. Place meat, onion, wine, undrained crushed tomatoes, stock, sauce, tomato paste and bay leaf in prepared dish. Bake, covered, for 1 1/2 hours or until meat is tender. Discard bay leaf.
3 Add mushrooms and broccoli to dish. Cook, covered, for 15 minutes.
4 To make Mustard Scone Topping: Place flour and salt in large bowl, rub in butter and mustard. Make a well in centre of mixture, add parsley and milk. Using a flat-bladed

for knife in a cutting action, mix until dough is soft and sticky. Turn onto lightly floured surface, knead gently with floured hands. Pat dough into a circle large enough to cover surface of casserole. Carefully place dough over casserole. Brush with extra milk. Bake for 25 minutes or until lightly browned and cooked through.

COOK'S FILE

Storage time: Meat filling can be cooked two days ahead. Prepare scone topping just before required.

BEEF BOURGUIGNON

Preparation time: 10 minutes
Total cooking time: 2 hours
Serves 6

1 kg topside or round steak
1/2 cup plain flour
salt and ground black pepper
3 rashers bacon
1/4 cup oil
12 pickling onions
200 g button mushrooms
1 cup good quality red wine
2 cups beef stock
1 teaspoon dried thyme
2 bay leaves

➤ TRIM MEAT of fat and sinew.
1 Cut meat into 2 cm cubes. Combine flour with salt and pepper on sheet of greaseproof paper. Toss meat lightly in seasoned flour; shake off excess.
2 Remove rind and excess fat from bacon, cut into 2 cm squares. Heat oil in large pan and cook bacon quickly in small batches over medium-high heat until browned; drain on paper towels. Remove excess fat from pan, add onions and brown over medium-high heat; drain. Add meat to pan in small batches, brown over medium-high heat; drain on paper towels.
3 Return bacon, meat and onions to pan. Add mushrooms, wine, stock, thyme and bay leaves; bring to the boil. Reduce heat. Simmer, covered, for 1 1/2 hours or until meat is very tender, stirring occasionally. Remove bay leaves before serving.

COOK'S FILE

Storage time: Will keep for up to three days in an airtight container in the refrigerator.
Hint: Serve with mashed potato and steamed green beans if liked.

1

2

3

LAMB

NAVARIN OF LAMB

Preparation time: 25 minutes
Total cooking time: 1 hour
  35 minutes
Serves 6

6 lamb noisettes
1/4 cup plain flour
salt and pepper
2 sticks celery
12 baby carrots
2 tablespoons oil
12 new potatoes
6 sprigs fresh thyme
1/4 cup chopped fresh parsley
2 medium onions, chopped
2 cloves garlic, crushed
1/3 cup plain flour, extra
2 1/2 cups chicken stock
1 cup good quality red wine
1/4 cup tomato paste

➤ TOSS LAMB in seasoned flour, shake off excess. Preheat oven to moderate 180°C (350°F/Gas Mark 4).
1 Cut celery diagonally into 2 cm pieces. Peel and trim carrots. Heat oil in heavy-based pan, cook lamb on both sides over medium-high heat until well browned. Remove from heat; drain on paper towels.
2 Place meat in 12-cup capacity greased baking dish. Top with celery, carrots, potatoes, thyme and parsley.
3 Add onions and garlic to pan and cook, stirring, until onion is soft. Add extra flour, stir 1 minute or until onion is coated. Add the stock, wine and tomato paste, stir over medium heat until mixture boils and thickens.
4 Pour sauce over lamb and vegetables. Cover with foil or lid. Bake for 1 1/4 hours or until lamb is tender.

COOK'S FILE

Storage time: This dish can be cooked one day ahead and reheated. Store, covered, in refrigerator.
Hints: Use four medium carrots, sliced, in place of baby carrots. A whole loin of lamb may be purchased and cut into noisettes. A boned leg of lamb, cut into 3 cm cubes, may be used as a substitute.

1

2

3

4

CURRIED LAMB CASSEROLE

Preparation time: 20 minutes
Total cooking time: 2 hours
    20 minutes
Serves 4

1 kg lamb neck chops
$1/4$ cup oil
1 clove garlic, crushed
1 tablespoon grated fresh ginger
1 large onion, chopped
1 teaspoon garam masala
1 teaspoon ground chilli powder
2 tablespoons Madras curry
    powder
2 cups chicken or lamb stock
1 tablespoon soft brown sugar

1 tablespoon tomato paste
3 whole cloves
1 large apple, peeled, chopped
$1/4$ cup sultanas

➤ TRIM MEAT of excess fat and sinew.

1 Heat 2 tablespoons oil in heavy-based pan. Cook meat quickly in small batches over medium heat until well browned. Drain on paper towels.

2 Heat remaining oil in pan. Add garlic, ginger and onion, stir over medium heat for 3 minutes or until soft. Add garam masala, chilli and curry powder. Cook, stirring, over medium heat for 2 minutes.

3 Return meat to pan, add stock, sugar, tomato paste, and cloves. Bring to boil, reduce heat, simmer. Cook covered for $1^{1}/_{2}$ hours or until meat is tender, stirring occasionally. Add apple and sultanas. Cook covered for a further 30 minutes. Serve with pilaf rice.

COOK'S FILE

Storage time: Curry paste may be made ahead of time and kept in an airtight container in the refrigerator. Suitable for freezing.

Hints: Lamb stock cubes are available from the supermarket. Alternatively, make your own stock using browned lamb bones. For an accompaniment, buy pappadums from the supermarket and prepare just before serving.

Variation: Add 400 mL coconut cream to make a rich creamy curry.

LAMB STEW WITH ROSEMARY DUMPLINGS

Preparation time: 25 minutes
Total cooking time: 2 hours
Serves 4

8 lamb neck chops
1/2 cup plain flour
salt and pepper
2 tablespoons oil
2 rashers bacon, finely chopped
1 large onion, sliced
2 cups beef stock
1/2 cup water
1 tablespoon chopped fresh thyme
2 medium carrots, thickly sliced
2 medium potatoes, chopped

Rosemary Dumplings
1 cup self-raising flour
20 g butter, chopped
1 teaspoon dried rosemary
1/3 cup milk

➤ TRIM MEAT of excess fat and sinew. Toss meat in flour, salt and pepper. Shake off excess.

1 Heat oil in a large heavy-based pan. Cook meat in batches, over medium-high heat, until well browned. Remove from pan. Add bacon to pan, cook until brown. Add onion, cook until onion is soft.

2 Return meat to pan. Add stock, water and thyme. Simmer covered over low heat for 30 minutes. Add carrots and potatoes, simmer for another hour.

3 To make Rosemary Dumplings: Sift flour into mixing bowl; add butter. Using fingertips, rub butter into flour until mixture is fine and crumbly. Stir in rosemary. Add almost all milk, mix to soft dough with a knife, adding more milk if necessary. Turn dough out onto lightly floured surface and knead gently for 1 minute or until smooth. Divide dough into eight portions, form into rough balls. Place dumplings into pan on top of hot meat mixture, cover, cook 15 minutes. Serve immediately.

COOK'S FILE

Storage time: Casserole may be made one day ahead. If you do this, make dumplings just before serving. Reheat casserole to simmering point just before adding dumplings.

HEARTY SHEPHERDS' PIE

Preparation time: 35 minutes
Total cooking time: 1 hour 40 minutes
Serves 6–8

1.5 kg leg lamb, boned
$1/2$ cup plain flour
salt and pepper
2 tablespoons oil
1 medium onion, chopped
1 cup beef stock
2 tablespoons tomato
   paste
2 medium carrots, sliced
1 cup frozen peas
1 tablespoon finely chopped
   fresh mint

Topping
4 large potatoes (1.5 kg),
   chopped
40 g butter
$1/4$ cup milk
$1/4$ teaspoon ground paprika

➤ LIGHTLY GREASE an 8-cup capacity casserole dish with oil or melted butter. Trim meat of excess fat and sinew. Cut meat into 1.5 cm cubes.

1 Combine flour, salt and pepper on a sheet of greaseproof paper. Toss meat gently in seasoned flour. Shake off excess. Heat oil in heavy-based pan. Cook meat in batches over medium-high heat until browned; drain on paper towels.

2 Add onion and cook, stirring, until soft. Return meat to pan. Add stock and tomato paste. Bring to boil; reduce heat. Simmer, covered, for 45 minutes, stirring occasionally. Add carrot, simmer 5 minutes.

3 Preheat oven to moderate 180°C (350°F/Gas Mark 4). Add peas to meat mixture. Stir over medium heat until mixture boils and thickens. Stir in mint. Spoon into prepared dish.

4 To make Topping: Add potatoes to large pan of boiling water. Simmer until tender. Drain. Mash slightly, add butter and milk, mash until smooth. Spread a small amount of mashed potato over the surface of meat. Spoon remaining potato mixture into a piping bag fitted with a 1.5 cm star nozzle. Pipe decoratively over lamb mixture. Sprinkle with paprika. Bake 25 minutes, or until potato is lightly browned. May be served with fresh crusty bread.

COOK'S FILE

Storage time: This dish can be made a day ahead and stored, covered, in refrigerator.
Hint: Ask the butcher to bone the leg of lamb. Minced lamb may be used as a substitute.

LAMB SHANKS IN TOMATO CHILLI SAUCE

Preparation time: 30 minutes
Total cooking time: 2½–2¾ hours
Serves 4

4 lamb shanks
¹/₂ cup plain flour
1 teaspoon curry powder
salt and pepper to taste
¹/₄ cup oil
1 large onion, finely chopped
1 small chilli, finely chopped
2 cloves garlic, crushed
4 tomatoes, peeled and chopped

2 teaspoons sugar
1 tablespoon tomato paste
1 cup dry white wine
¹/₄ cup finely chopped fresh parsley
¹/₄ cup basil leaves, shredded

➤ TRIM LAMB shanks of any excess fat and sinew.

1 Combine flour, curry powder, salt and pepper in plastic bag. Toss lamb shanks lightly in seasoned flour; shake off excess.

2 Heat half the oil in pan, brown shanks in batches over medium-high heat, drain on paper towels. Place lamb in large, shallow, ovenproof dish.

3 Wipe out pan, heat remaining oil and stir-fry onion with chilli and garlic for 5 minutes or until onion is tender. Add tomatoes, sugar and tomato paste, cook 2 minutes. Add wine, season with salt and pepper to taste. Pour sauce over shanks. Cover dish tightly. Bake in warm 160°C (315°F/Gas Mark 2–3) oven for 2–2 ¹/₂ hours or until tender. Ensure lid is tight to retain moisture. Serve with sprinkling of parsley and basil.

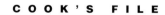

COOK'S FILE

Storage time: May be prepared up to two days ahead and stored, covered in refrigerator.

1

2

3

KIDNEY AND BACON RAGOUT

Preparation time: 40 minutes
Total cooking time: 35–40 minutes
Serves 4

8 lamb's kidneys
45 g butter or 1 tablespoon oil
200 g bacon, cut into 5 cm
    pieces
2 medium onions, finely chopped
4 small tomatoes, peeled and
    cut into quarters
salt and pepper
1 tablespoon plain flour
1/3 cup chicken stock or water
2 teaspoons dry sherry or
    Madeira
1/4 cup finely chopped parsley

➤ PREHEAT OVEN to moderate 180°C (350°F/Gas Mark 4). Peel skin from kidneys. Cut kidneys in half, remove the core and any excess fat.

1 Heat butter or oil in heavy-based frying pan. Add kidneys, cook over medium heat 3–4 minutes or until colour has changed. Strain juices from kidneys in a sieve. Discard juices.

2 Place bacon and onion in same pan. Cook over medium heat 5–10 minutes or until tender. Add tomatoes, salt and pepper; cook further 5 minutes. Remove from heat. Transfer mixture to 5-cup capacity casserole dish.

3 Blend flour with a little water to make a thin paste. Add remaining water or stock. Add flour mixture, kidneys and sherry or Madeira to casserole, mix well. Bake uncovered 15–20 minutes or until kidneys are cooked. Sprinkle with parsley. Serve.

COOK'S FILE

Storage time: This dish is best eaten on the day it is made.

1

2

3

HERB LAMB TRIANGLES

Preparation time: 40 minutes
Total cooking time: 45 minutes
Makes 8

1 medium potato, peeled
1 tablespoon oil
2 onions, sliced
500 g lamb mince
$^1/_4$ cup shredded fresh basil
2 tablespoons chopped
   fresh mint
2 teaspoons ground cumin
$^1/_4$ teaspoon ground
   cardamom
2 tablespoons currants
$^1/_4$ teaspoon caster sugar
$^1/_3$ cup good quality white wine
1 tablespoon tomato paste
1 cup beef stock
1 teaspoon cornflour
1 tablespoon water
$^1/_3$ cup pine nuts, toasted
12 sheets filo pastry
60 g butter, melted
1$^1/_2$ teaspoons poppy seeds

➤ PREHEAT OVEN to hot 210°C
(415°F/Gas Mark 6–7). Cut potato
into 1 cm cubes.

1 Heat oil in pan, add onions. Cook,
stirring, over medium heat until soft.
Add mince; cook, stirring, until mince
is well browned. Use a fork to break
up any lumps. Add potato, basil, mint,
cumin, cardamom and currants. Cook,
stirring, 2–3 minutes until fragrant.

2 Stir in sugar, wine, paste and stock.
Bring to boil, reduce heat. Simmer for
5 minutes, stirring occasionally, or
until slightly thickened. Blend cornflour and water in small bowl until
smooth. Add to pan. Simmer over
medium heat, stirring until thickened.
Add pine nuts, remove from heat.

3 Lay three sheets of pastry on work
surface. Brush each sheet with butter.
Lay sheets on top of each other. Cut
pastry in half lengthways. Place $^1/_2$ cup
mince mixture at one end of each strip.
Fold each strip of pastry along length
forming a triangle. Repeat with remaining pastry, butter and filling until all
ingredients are used.

4 Place triangles on a greased oven
tray. Brush each triangle with some
extra butter and sprinkle tops with
poppy seeds. Bake 25 minutes or until
golden and crisp. Serve with minted
yoghurt if desired.

COOK'S FILE

Storage time: Cook recipe on day of
serving. May be frozen for up to one
month.
Hint: Use chopped raisins or sultanas
in place of currants.

LAMB MEATBALLS IN CAPSICUM SAUCE

Preparation time: 35 minutes
Total cooking time: 1 hour 15 minutes
Serves 4

750 g lamb mince
1 medium onion, grated
2 teaspoons Dijon mustard
1 tablespoon chopped fresh
  chives
1 tablespoon chopped fresh
  parsley
1 egg
1 cup fresh white breadcrumbs
plain flour
2 tablespoons oil
2 large red capsicum
1 tablespoon balsamic vinegar
2 cloves garlic, crushed
¹/₂ cup lemon juice
¹/₄ teaspoon sambal oelek
¹/₂ cup good quality red wine
¹/₂ teaspoon caster sugar

➤ PREHEAT OVEN to moderate 180°C (350°F/Gas Mark 4).
1 Combine mince, onion, mustard, chives, parsley, egg and breadcrumbs in medium bowl; mix well. Roll tablespoons of mixture into balls.
2 Toss meatballs in flour, shake off excess. Heat oil in heavy-based pan, cook meatballs over medium heat, turning occasionally, until browned all over; drain on paper towels. Place meatballs in an 8-cup capacity casserole dish.
3 Cut capsicum into quarters, remove seeds and membrane. Grill, skin-side up, until skin blisters and blackens. Cool slightly, peel away skin. Place capsicum in food processor bowl. Process until smooth.
4 Combine puréed capsicum with vinegar, garlic, lemon juice, sambal oelek, wine and sugar. Pour over meatballs. Cover, bake 45 minutes or until meatballs are tender.

COOK'S FILE

Storage time: Can be made a day ahead, stored, covered, in refrigerator and reheated.
Hints: Beef or chicken mince can be used instead of lamb. Make more breadcrumbs than required and store in one-cup quantities in freezer.

1

2

3

4

SPANISH LAMB

Preparation time: 20 minutes
Total cooking time: 1 hour 35 minutes
Serves 4–6

30 g butter
1 tablespoon olive oil
1 kg diced lamb
2 large red onions, chopped
1 tablespoon plain flour
1 teaspoon ground cumin
1/2 cup dry sherry
1/2 cup orange juice
1/2 cup chicken stock
2 teaspoons grated orange rind

➤ PREHEAT OVEN to warm 160°C (315°F/Gas Mark 2–3).

1 Heat butter and oil in large pan until butter is foaming. Add diced lamb and cook 3-5 minutes or until lamb is browned all over. Remove with a slotted spoon and place in a casserole dish.

2 Add onion to the pan and cook slowly for 3 minutes or until soft. Add flour and cumin. Stir over low heat for 2 minutes or until flour mixture is lightly golden. Add combined sherry, juice and stock, stirring until mixture, is smooth. Stir constantly over medium heat for 3 minutes or until mixture boils and thickens; boil for another minute; remove from heat. Stir in orange rind.

3 Pour sauce over meat and stir gently to combine. Cover and cook for 1¼ hours or until meat is tender. Serve with boiled rice.

COOK'S FILE

Storage time: This recipe can be prepared up to two days in advance.
Hints: Diced lamb is now available from most butchers. If unavailable, ask the butcher to bone and dice a small leg of lamb. Diced veal or pork can be used in place of lamb. Greengrocers often refer to red onions as Spanish onions.

SWEET CURRY LAMB PIE

Preparation time: 30 minutes
Total cooking time: 2 hours
Serves 8

750g diced lamb
1/2 cup plain flour
2 tablespoons oil
2 onions, sliced
1 tablespoon curry powder
1 3/4 cups beef stock
2 apples, peeled, cut into
    2 cm pieces
2/3 cup sultanas
1 tablespoon cornflour

2 tablespoons water
10 sheets filo pastry
60g butter, melted
3/4 cup walnuts, chopped
1/2 cup icing sugar
1 teaspoon ground cinnamon

➤ PREHEAT OVEN to hot 210°C (415°F/Gas mark 6–7).

1 Toss lamb in flour, shake off excess. Heat oil, brown meat; drain.

2 Add onion, cook 5 minutes. Add curry powder, cook 1 minute. Return meat to pan. Add stock, bring to boil. Reduce heat; simmer covered 1 hour, stirring occasionally. Simmer uncovered for 10 minutes. Add apple, sultanas and blended cornflour and water. Stir over medium heat until thickened. Cool.

3 Brush 5 sheets filo pastry with butter. Fold in half lengthways. Arrange sheets, overlapping, over base of 30 cm round tray. Sprinkle with one-third of combined walnuts, sugar and cinnamon, top with lamb. Cover with remaining buttered pastry, overlapping, tucking edges underneath. Brush top with butter. Sprinkle with remaining walnut mixture. Bake 30 minutes.

COOK'S FILE

Storage time: Can be made a day ahead. Store, civered, in refrigerator and reheat when required.

Sweet Curry Lamb Pie (top) and Spanish Lamb.

GREEK LAMB AND MACARONI

Preparation time: 25 minutes
Total cooking time: 50 minutes
Serves 4–6

750 g boneless lamb
¼ cup olive oil
2 large onions, chopped
2 cloves garlic, crushed
410 g can tomatoes
¼ cup tomato paste
1 cup beef stock
2 tablespoons red
wine vinegar
1 tablespoon soft
brown sugar

1 teaspoon dried oregano
200 g macaroni
125 g pecorino cheese, coarsely
grated

➤ TRIM MEAT of excess fat and sinew.
1 Cut meat into 1 cm cubes. Heat oil in heavy-based pan. Cook meat quickly, in small batches, over medium-high heat until well browned; drain on paper towels.
2 Remove excess oil from pan. Add onions and garlic. Cook over low heat until onions are soft. Add tomatoes, tomato paste, stock, vinegar, sugar and oregano.
3 Return meat to pan and bring to the boil. Reduce heat; simmer, covered,

for 20 minutes, stirring occasionally.
4 Add pasta, stir to combine. Bring to boil, reduce heat. Simmer, covered, 15 minutes or until meat and pasta are tender. Serve, topped with cheese, in individual bowls or a large bowl.

COOK'S FILE

Storage time: Dish can be made day before required.
Hint: Beef can be used in place of lamb in this recipe.

LAMB WITH BEANS AND LEMON

Preparation time: 25 minutes
  + overnight soaking
Total cooking time: 2 hours 15 minutes
Serves 6

1 cup dried haricot beans
1 tablespoon olive oil
1 large onion, sliced
2 cloves garlic, crushed
425 g can tomatoes, chopped
2 tablespoons sherry
1 tablespoon chopped fresh thyme
2 tablespoons finely chopped
  parsley
1 large lemon
2 cups vegetable stock

2 kg leg of lamb
1 tablespoon olive oil, extra
black pepper
12 small button squash

➤ SOAK BEANS in a large bowl of cold water overnight. Drain, rinse and place in a large pan; cover with cold water. Bring to the boil, reduce heat and simmer uncovered for 45 minutes, until just tender. Drain and cool.

1 Preheat oven to moderate 180°C (350°F/Gas Mark 4). Heat oil in a medium pan. Cook onion and garlic over medium heat 3 minutes or until soft. Add tomatoes, sherry and herbs, stir to combine.

2 Place beans in a large baking dish, add tomato mixture. Using a vegetable peeler, cut 3 x 2 cm strips of peel from lemon, avoiding white pith. Add to baking dish, with 2 tablespoons lemon juice and half the stock. Stir mixture to combine evenly.

3 Trim meat of excess fat and sinew. Place in dish on top of the beans, brush with oil and sprinkle with freshly ground black pepper. Bake for 1 hour, remove from oven. Turn meat over, add remaining stock and squash to dish. Bake a further 30 minutes, until meat is cooked and squash is tender. To serve, remove lamb from dish and carve into slices. Serve with beans and squash.

COOK'S FILE

Storage time: This dish can be made a day in advance. Reheat gently to serve.

1

2

3

45

PORK

PORK VINDALOO

Preparation time: 20 minutes
Total cooking time: 1 hour 45 minutes
Serves 4

1 kg pork fillets

Vindaloo Mixture
**2 tablespoons grated fresh
   ginger
4 cloves garlic, chopped
3 small red chillies, chopped
2 teaspoons ground turmeric
2 teaspoons ground cardamom
4 whole cloves
6 peppercorns
1 teaspoon ground cinnamon
1 tablespoon ground coriander
1 tablespoon cumin seeds
1/2 cup lemon juice**

**1/4 cup oil
2 teaspoons brown mustard seeds
2 1/2 cups water**

➤ TRIM MEAT of excess fat and sinew. Cut pork into 2 cm cubes.

1 To make Vindaloo Mixture: Place ginger, garlic, chilli, turmeric, cardamom, cloves, peppercorns, cinnamon, coriander, cumin seeds and lemon juice in food processor. Process 20 seconds or until all ingredients are combined and mixture is quite smooth.
2 Heat oil in heavy-based pan, add meat in small batches, cook quickly over medium heat until browned. Return all meat to pan.
3 Add Vindaloo Mixture and mustard seeds, cook stirring for 2 minutes.
4 Add water. Bring to boil, reduce heat, simmer. Cook, covered, 1 1/2 hours or until meat is tender. Serve with rice and pappadums.

COOK'S FILE

Storage time: Vindaloo paste may be made ahead of time and stored in an airtight container in the refrigerator.
Hints: Bottled vindaloo paste is available in supermarkets.
Pappadums can be brushed lightly with oil and microwaved briefly.
Variations: Beef or chicken may be substituted for pork in this recipe. Cooking time for each will vary.

PORK AND VEAL CASSEROLE

Preparation time: 20 minutes
Total cooking time: 1 hour 20 minutes
Serves 4–6

500 g boneless cubed veal
500 g boneless cubed pork
20 g butter
2 tablespoons oil
2 medium onions,
   chopped
2 tablespoons plain flour
2 cups chicken stock
1/2 cup brandy
2 tablespoons redcurrant jelly

1/4 cup fresh rosemary leaves
250 g button mushrooms

➤ PREHEAT OVEN to warm 160°C (315°F/Gas Mark 2–3). Trim meat of excess fat and sinew.

1 Heat butter and oil in large heavy-based pan. Cook meat quickly, in small batches, over medium-high heat until well browned; drain on paper towels. Place in large casserole dish. Add onion to pan. Stir over low heat 2 minutes or until well browned. Add flour and cook, stirring, 2 minutes.

2 Add stock and brandy to pan, stirring until sauce is smooth. Stir 3 minutes over low heat until sauce boils and thickens. Stir in redcurrant

jelly and rosemary leaves; simmer uncovered for 2 minutes.

3 Pour sauce over meat in casserole dish. Stir gently to combine. Cover and bake for 40 minutes. Remove from oven. Add mushrooms, stir to combine. Cover and return to oven for further 30 minutes, or until meat is cooked and tender.

COOK'S FILE

Storage time: Dish can be made one to two days before required.
Hint: All veal or all pork can be used in this recipe. This recipe uses cubed meat that the butcher has prepared. Any boneless meat can be used and cut into 3 cm cubes.

PORK WITH GINGER AND APRICOTS

Preparation time: 20 minutes
Total cooking time: 55 minutes
Serves 4–6

750 g pork fillet
2 tablespoons oil
2 tablespoons shredded fresh
   ginger
8 spring onions, sliced
125 g dried apricots, chopped
1 cup chicken stock
1/2 cup orange juice

2 tablespoons honey
2 teaspoons finely grated orange
   rind
1 tablespoon cornflour
2 cinnamon sticks

➤ PREHEAT OVEN to warm 160°C (315°F/Gas Mark 2–3). Trim meat of excess fat and sinew.

1 Slice meat into flat thin strips. Heat oil in heavy-based pan. Cook meat quickly, in small batches, over medium-high heat until well browned; drain on paper towels.

2 Add ginger, onions and apricots to pan; cook over low heat 1 minute. Stir

in combined stock, orange juice, honey and rind and simmer for 2 minutes.

3 Blend cornflour with a little cold water in small bowl or jug until smooth. Add to mixture in pan, stir over medium heat 3 minutes or until sauce boils and thickens. Simmer for 2 minutes. Return meat to pan; stir to combine. Transfer mixture to casserole dish. Add cinnamon sticks; cover, cook 35 minutes or until meat is tender. Remove cinnamon sticks.

COOK'S FILE

Storage time: Dish can be made day before required. Refrigerate.

Pork and Veal Casserole (top) and Pork with Ginger and Apricots.

PORK AND VEAL PIE

Preparation time: 30 minutes +
  1 hour standing
Total cooking time: 45 minutes
Serves 6

Filling
15 g dried Chinese mushrooms
1/2 cup boiling water
500 g pork and veal mince
200 g chicken livers, chopped
4 rashers bacon, finely chopped
2 eggs, lightly beaten
2 teaspoons ground coriander
1 teaspoon mixed spice
2 cloves garlic, crushed
1 tablespoon chopped fresh
  thyme
1/2 cup pistachio nuts, chopped
2 tablespoons brandy
1 tablespoon sherry
1/2 cup cream

Pastry
2 1/4 cups plain flour
125 g butter, chopped
1/2 cup iced water
1 egg, lightly beaten, extra

➤ SOAK MUSHROOMS in boiling water until soft. Drain and chop, reserve liquid.

1 To make Filling: Combine mince, livers, bacon, eggs, coriander, mixed spice, garlic, thyme, pistachios, brandy, sherry, cream and mushrooms in large mixing bowl. Using hands, mix well. Cover with plastic wrap. Stand 1 hour.

2 To make Pastry: Place flour and butter in food processor bowl. Process for 20 seconds or until mixture is fine and crumbly. Add almost all the water and process until mixture comes together, adding more water if necessary. Turn onto lightly floured surface, press together until smooth. Roll out two-thirds of pastry to line greased 23 cm pie dish. Wrap remaining pastry in plastic, refrigerate pie dish and pastry for 20 minutes. Place filling in pastry shell. Preheat oven to hot 210°C (415°F/Gas Mark 6–7). Brush pastry edges with beaten egg. Roll out remaining pastry to cover pie dish.

3 Trim pastry edge with sharp knife. Cut three steam holes in top of pie. Brush with egg. Bake 45 minutes or until golden.

COOK'S FILE

Storage time: Pie can be made up to two days ahead. Serve cold or reheat gently in moderate oven 15 minutes

1

2

3

4

QUICK PORK CASSEROLE

Preparation time: 30 minutes
Total cooking time: 45 minutes
Serves 6

1 medium eggplant, cut into
    2 cm slices
900 g pork fillets
2 tablespoons oil
1 large onion,
    chopped
2 cloves garlic, crushed
1 large red capsicum, cut into
    3 cm squares
1 large green capsicum, cut into
    3 cm squares
3 medium zucchini, cut into
    2 cm slices

810 g can peeled tomatoes,
    crushed
$^{1}/_{2}$ cup good quality white wine
1 teaspoon dried oregano
1 teaspoon dried thyme
2 teaspoons dried basil

➤ PLACE EGGPLANT on a board in a single layer.

1 Sprinkle eggplant generously with salt. Leave for 20 minutes, then rinse and pat dry with paper towels.

2 Trim meat of excess fat and sinew, cut into 2 cm cubes. Heat oil in a large pan. Cook meat quickly, in small batches, over medium-high heat until browned; drain on paper towels.

3 Add onion and garlic to same pan, cook for 2 minutes or until tender. Add capsicum, cook for another 5 minutes, stirring occasionally.

4 Return meat to pan with remaining ingredients; bring to the boil. Reduce heat to a simmer; cook, uncovered, 30 minutes or until meat is tender, stirring occasionally. May be served with fettuccine or pasta spirals.

COOK'S FILE

Storage time: Will keep up to one day in airtight container in refrigerator.
Hint: Chicken thigh fillets may be substituted for pork if desired.

ITALIAN SAUSAGE CASSEROLE

Preparation time: 15 minutes
Cooking time: 45 minutes
Serves 4

3 cups milk
30 g butter
1 cup (60 g) fine or coarse
   polenta
1/2 cup grated parmesan cheese
1 tablespoon oil
1 clove garlic, crushed
1 large red onion, cut in 8 wedges
1 medium red capsicum, chopped
410 g can peeled tomatoes,
   chopped
2 tablespoons tomato paste
1 tablespoon Worcestershire
   sauce
250 g salami, chopped
125 g mozzarella cheese, grated
1/2 cup grated parmesan cheese,
   extra

➤ PREHEAT OVEN to hot 210°C (415°F/Gas Mark 6–7).

1 Heat milk and butter in large heavy-based pan. Stir over medium heat until simmering.

2 Add polenta gradually to pan, stirring constantly over medium heat until mixture thickens and leaves the sides of the pan. Stir in parmesan. Spoon the mixture evenly over the base of a large ovenproof dish.

3 Heat oil in a heavy-based pan. Add garlic, onion and capsicum. Cook over medium heat for 3 minutes or until soft. Add tomatoes, tomato paste, Worcestershire sauce and salami. Bring to boil, reduce heat, simmer 10 minutes. Pour tomato mixture over polenta.

4 Combine mozzarella and extra parmesan in small bowl. Sprinkle over tomato mixture. Bake for 30 minutes or until golden. Serve with green salad.

COOK'S FILE

Storage time: Cook this dish just before serving.

Hint: Polenta is also referred to as coarse cornmeal and is available in health food stores and some supermarkets in the health food section.

Variation: Other continental sausages are suitable for this recipe.

1

2

3

4

BACON, HERB AND VEGETABLE PIE

Preparation time: 25 minutes
Total cooking time: 55 minutes
Serves 6

30 g butter
1 clove garlic, crushed
1 medium onion, chopped
1 tablespoon plain flour
100 g button mushrooms, halved
150 g bacon off the bone, chopped
1 large carrot, chopped
1 parsnip, chopped
2 leeks, thinly sliced
1¼ cups cream

1 tablespoon chopped fresh rosemary
2 sheets ready-rolled puff pastry
1 egg, lightly beaten

➤ PREHEAT OVEN to moderate 180°C (350°F/Gas Mark 4).
1 Heat butter in heavy-based pan, add garlic and onion. Cook over medium heat for 3 minutes or until golden. Add flour, stir 1 minute.
2 Add mushrooms and bacon, cook for 5 minutes. Add carrot, parsnip and leek. Gradually stir in cream and rosemary. Bring to boil, reduce heat, cover, simmer 15 minutes or until vegetables are tender.
3 Spoon mixture into 23 cm pie dish. Cut each pastry sheet into twelve

equal strips; weave strips into tight lattice pattern, brushing with egg. Carefully lift pastry and place over pie. Trim edges with a sharp knife. Brush top of pastry with egg. Bake for 25 minutes or until golden. Serve with a crisp green salad or noodles.

COOK'S FILE

Storage time: Cook this dish just before serving.
Hints: Bacon off the bone is available from butchers and delicatessens.
When preparing leeks, remove the outer leaves and cut off the root section. Rinse thoroughly in cold water making sure all grit is removed.
Variation: Ham off the bone may be used in this recipe.

HEARTY BACON AND BEAN STEWPOT

Preparation time: 25 minutes
Total cooking time: 40 minutes
Serves 4–6

200 g piece of speck
2 tablespoons oil
2 small leeks,
   thinly sliced
2 tablespoons plain flour
2 cups chicken stock
4 medium potatoes (800 g),
   peeled, cut into 1 cm cubes
3 large carrots, cut into 1 cm
   cubes
410 g can red kidney beans,
   rinsed and drained
1/2 cup finely chopped parsley
1/2 teaspoon freshly ground
   black pepper

➤ REMOVE RIND from speck.
1 Cut speck into 1 cm cubes. Place speck in large pan; cook over low heat until crisp. Remove from pan and drain on paper towels. Remove excess fat from pan.
2 Heat oil in pan, add leeks, cook for 5 minutes until soft. Add flour to pan. Stir over low heat for 2 minutes or until flour mixture is lightly golden.
3 Add stock gradually to pan, stirring until mixture is smooth. Stir constantly over medium heat for 3 minutes or until mixture boils and thickens; boil further 1 minute. Reduce heat; simmer.
4 When at simmering point, add potatoes, carrots and drained speck; cover and cook gently over medium heat 20 minutes or until potatoes and carrots are tender.
5 Add beans, parsley and pepper, stir to combine. Cook over low heat for 5 minutes. Serve with a green vegetable such as steamed broccoli or green beans.

COOK'S FILE

Storage time: This dish is best eaten on the day it is made.
Hints: Any canned beans can be used in this recipe. Speck is available from butchers and also delicatessens. If you don't like its strong taste, thick bacon rashers with rind removed can be used to replace speck.

1

2

3

4

5

1

2

3

4

BOSTON BAKED BEANS

Preparation time: 25 minutes +
  overnight soaking
Total cooking time: 1 hour
  35 minutes
Serves 4–6

375 g dried cannellini beans
1 whole ham hock
2 medium onions,
  chopped
1/2 cup tomato juice
2 tablespoons tomato paste
1 tablespoon Worcestershire
  sauce
1 tablespoon molasses
1 teaspoon French mustard
1/4 cup soft brown sugar

➤ PLACE BEANS in large basin. Cover with cold water and leave to soak 6–8 hours or overnight.

1 Preheat oven to warm 160°C (315°F/Gas Mark 2–3). Drain beans; place in large saucepan. Add ham hock; cover with cold water. Bring to the boil; reduce heat. Simmer, covered, for 25 minutes or until beans are tender. Remove from heat, remove ham hock, set aside to cool. Drain beans; reserve 1 cup of cooking liquid.

2 Trim ham hock of all fat and sinew; chop meat and discard bone.

3 Place beans and ham meat in an 8-cup capacity casserole dish. Add the reserved liquid, onions, tomato juice, tomato paste, Worcestershire sauce, molasses, mustard and sugar. Mix gently to combine.

4 Cover and cook for 1 hour. Serve accompanied by hot buttered toast.

COOK'S FILE

Storage time: Beans can be prepared two or three days before required.
Hint: Any dried bean can be used. Beans can be prepared by quick soaking method. Place beans in saucepan, cover with hot water and bring slowly to the boil. Remove from heat; leave in water for one hour. Drain.

PORK AND PINEAPPLE CASSEROLE

Preparation time: 20 minutes
Total cooking time: 1 hour 45 minutes
Serves 4–6

750 g boneless pork
3/4 cup cornflour
1/2 teaspoon five spice powder
2 tablespoons oil
1 large onion, finely chopped
440 g can pineapple pieces in natural juice
1 cup chicken stock
1 tablespoon tomato paste
1 tablespoon soft brown sugar
1 tablespoon white vinegar
1 small green capsicum, finely chopped

➤ PREHEAT OVEN to warm 160°C (315°F/Gas Mark 2–3). Trim meat of fat and sinew. Cut into 3 cm cubes.

1 Combine cornflour and five spice powder on a sheet of greaseproof paper, toss meat lightly in seasoned flour; shake off excess. Heat oil in heavy-based pan. Cook pork quickly, in small batches, over medium-high heat until well browned; drain on paper towels. Transfer meat to an 8-cup capacity casserole dish.

2 Add onion to pan and cook over medium-high heat for 2 minutes. Drain pineapple, reserve juice. Add onion and pineapple pieces to pork in casserole dish.

3 Pour over. combined pineapple juice, stock, paste, brown sugar and vinegar. Cover and cook for 1 hour. Add capsicum, stir to combine and cook for another 30 minutes.

COOK'S FILE

Storage time: This recipe can be made day before required.

1

2

3

POULTRY & GAME

CHICKEN AND BACON WITH GLAZED CARROTS

Preparation time: 40 minutes
Total cooking time: 1 hour 10 minutes
Serves 6

1.4 kg chicken
1/4 cup plain flour
1 teaspoon ground black pepper
salt
20 spring onions
4 bacon rashers (100 g)
2 tablespoons olive oil
20 g butter
225 g button mushrooms, halved
30 g butter, extra
2 cloves garlic, crushed
1 tablespoon chopped fresh thyme
1 tablespoon plain flour, extra
3/4 cup good quality white wine
1 cup chicken stock

Glazed Carrots
2 large carrots
1 large onion
25 g butter
1 teaspoon sugar
1/2 cup water

➤ TRIM CHICKEN of excess fat and sinew. Cut chicken into 8 pieces. Combine flour, pepper and salt on greaseproof paper. Toss chicken in seasoned flour; shake off excess. Cut spring onions into 7 cm lengths. Cut bacon in 3 cm pieces.
1 Heat oil in pan. Cook spring onions over medium heat 2–3 minutes. Remove from pan. Drain on paper towels. Add butter and mushrooms to pan. Cook over medium heat 4 minutes. Remove from pan, drain on paper towels.
2 Heat extra butter in pan. Cook bacon, garlic and thyme over medium heat 5 minutes. Brown chicken in small batches. Remove from pan. Add extra flour; cook, stirring, 5 minutes. Return chicken to pan. Add wine and stock. Bring to boil, reduce heat, simmer 45 minutes or until chicken is tender.
3 To make Glazed Carrots: Cut carrots in 1 x 3 cm pieces. Cut onion into thin slices. Combine butter, sugar and water in pan. Stir over medium heat until butter has melted and sugar is dissolved. Add carrots and onion. Bring to boil, reduce heat, simmer until liquid is completely reduced. Stir occasionally to prevent burning. Remove from heat. Add mushrooms and spring onions to chicken. Stir until heated through. Serve casserole topped with Glazed Carrots.

COOK'S FILE

Storage time: This dish is best eaten the day it is made.

CHICKEN AND APPLE CURRY

Preparation time: 20 minutes
Total cooking time: 1 hour 5 minutes
Serves 4–6

1 kg chicken wings
1/4 cup oil
1 large onion, sliced
1 tablespoon curry powder
1 large carrot, chopped
1 stick celery, sliced
400 mL can coconut cream
1 cup chicken stock
2 medium green apples,
    chopped
1 tablespoon finely chopped
    fresh coriander
1/4 cup sultanas
1/2 cup roasted peanuts

➤ WASH AND PAT dry chicken wings.

1 Tuck wing tips to underside.

2 Heat 2 tablespoons oil in large heavy-based pan, add chicken in small batches. Cook quickly over medium heat 5 minutes or until well browned on both sides. Drain on paper towels.

3 Heat remaining oil in pan. Add onion and curry powder, stir over medium heat 3 minutes or until soft.

4 Return chicken to pan. Add carrot, celery, coconut cream and stock; bring to boil. Reduce heat, simmer. Cook, covered, 30 minutes. Add apples, coriander and sultanas and cook for a further 20 minutes or until chicken is tender, stirring occasionally. Serve sprinkled with roasted peanuts.

COOK'S FILE

Storage time: Cook this dish up to two days in advance.

Hints: Coconut cream is available in cans or tetra packs from supermarkets and delicatessens.

Serve curry with steamed or boiled rice. Sliced bananas can be served with a sprinkling of lemon juice and rolled in desiccated coconut. For refreshing the palate, mix a peeled, chopped cucumber into 1/2 cup plain yoghurt and serve.

Variations: Pear may be used instead of apple in this recipe.

Curry paste may be used instead of curry powder.

CHICKEN CHASSEUR

Preparation time: 20 minutes
Total cooking time: 1 hour 45 minutes
Serves 4

1 kg chicken thigh fillets
2 tablespoons oil
1 clove garlic, crushed
1 large onion, sliced
100 g button mushrooms, sliced
1 teaspoon chopped fresh thyme
400 g can peeled tomatoes,
    chopped

¹/₄ cup chicken stock
¹/₄ cup good quality white wine
1 tablespoon tomato paste

➤ PREHEAT OVEN to moderate
180°C (350°F/Gas Mark 4). Trim
chicken of excess fat and sinew.
1 Heat oil in heavy-based frying pan.
Cook chicken quickly in batches over
medium heat 3–4 minutes or until
well browned. Drain on paper towels.
Transfer chicken to 8-cup capacity
ovenproof casserole dish.
2 Add garlic, onion and mushrooms
to pan. Cook over medium heat for

5 minutes or until soft. Add to chicken
with thyme and tomatoes.
3 Pour over combined stock, wine
and tomato paste. Cover. Bake for
1 hour 15 minutes or until chicken is
tender. May be served with steamed
vegetables and baby potatoes.

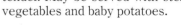

COOK'S FILE

Storage time: This dish may be
cooked a day ahead and stored in an
airtight container in the refrigerator.
Variations: Chicken maryland may be
used in this recipe. Red wine may be
used in place of white wine.

1

2

3

MOROCCAN CHICKEN

Preparation time: 20 minutes +
  2 hours marinating
Total cooking time: 1 hour 25 minutes
Serves 4

8 large chicken drumsticks
3 cloves garlic, crushed
1 teaspoon grated fresh ginger
1 teaspoon ground turmeric
2 teaspoons ground cumin
1 teaspoon ground cardamom
1 teaspoon finely grated lemon
  rind
2 tablespoons oil

1 medium onion, sliced
2 cups chicken stock
6 pitted dates, chopped
¹/₃ cup shredded coconut

➤ TRIM CHICKEN of excess fat and
sinew. Place chicken in a large bowl.
1 Combine garlic, ginger, turmeric,
cumin, cardamom and rind in small
bowl. Add to chicken, stir to completely
coat. Cover and marinate for 2 hours.
2 Preheat oven to moderate 180°C
(350°F/Gas Mark 4). Heat oil in a
heavy-based frying pan. Cook chicken
over medium heat until well browned;
drain on paper towels. Place chicken
in an ovenproof casserole dish.

3 Add onion to pan, cook, stirring for
5 minutes until soft. Add cooked onion,
stock, dates and coconut to casserole
dish. Cover and bake 1 hour 15 minutes or until chicken is tender, stirring
occasionally. May be served with
jasmine rice and stir-fried vegetables.

COOK'S FILE

Storage time: The chicken may be
left to marinate overnight in refrigerator. This recipe can be made the day
before and stored in airtight container
in refrigerator. Also suitable to freeze.
Variations: Dried apricots or prunes
are great alternatives to dates. Beef
or fish may be used for this recipe.

1

2

3

CHICKEN IN RICH MUSHROOM SAUCE

Preparation time: 40 minutes
Total cooking time: 1 hour 10 minutes
  Serves 4

1.4 kg chicken
1 medium onion, sliced
2 whole cloves
8–10 peppercorns
1 teaspoon salt
3 cups water
90 g butter
500 g mushrooms, sliced
2 cloves garlic, crushed
2 tablespoons plain flour
$^{1}/_{2}$ cup cream
1 tablespoon French mustard
1 cup grated cheddar cheese
$^{1}/_{2}$ cup stale breadcrumbs
$^{1}/_{4}$ cup finely chopped fresh
  parsley

➤ PREHEAT OVEN to moderate 180°C (350°F/Gas Mark 4). Trim chicken. Cut into 10 portions.

1 Place chicken, onion, spices and salt into 8-cup capacity ovenproof dish. Cover with water. Bake 30 minutes. Remove chicken. Strain liquid into bowl, reserving 2 cups. Melt half the butter in frying pan. Add mushrooms, cook until soft. Add garlic, cook 2 minutes. Transfer to bowl.

2 Melt remaining butter in pan. Add flour, cook 2 minutes. Gradually add reserved liquid, stir until smooth. Bring to boil. Remove from heat, stir in cream, mustard and mushrooms.

3 Return chicken and sauce to dish. Sprinkle with combined cheese, breadcrumbs and parsley. Bake 30 minutes.

COOK'S FILE

Storage time: Prepare this dish up to one day ahead. Cover, refrigerate.

1

2

3

COQ AU VIN

Preparation time: 20 minutes
Total cooking time: 1 hour
Serves 6

2 kg chicken pieces
plain flour
salt and pepper
2 tablespoons oil
1 tablespoon oil, extra
4 bacon rashers, sliced
10 small pickling onions
1 clove garlic, crushed

1½ cups good quality red wine
1½ cups chicken stock
¼ cup tomato paste
250 g small button mushrooms

➤ COAT CHICKEN in seasoned flour, shake off excess.
1 Heat oil in heavy-based pan. Cook chicken quickly in small batches until well browned; drain on paper towels.
2 Heat extra oil in deep heavy-based pan. Add bacon, onions and garlic; cook, stirring, until onions are browned. Add chicken, wine, stock and paste. Bring to boil and reduce heat and simmer, covered, 30 minutes.
3 Add mushrooms, stir to combine and simmer, uncovered, for a further 10 minutes, or until chicken is tender and sauce has thickened slightly. May be served sprinkled with chopped fresh herbs.

COOK'S FILE

Storage time: This dish can be cooked two days ahead and reheated. Store, covered, in refrigerator.
Variation: A jointed 1.5 kg chicken can be used instead of chicken pieces for this recipe.

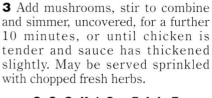

CHICKEN AND PINE NUT ROLLS IN TOMATO SAUCE

Preparation time: 40 minutes
Total cooking time: 35 minutes
Serves 4–6

6 chicken breast fillets
¾ cup fresh wholemeal
   breadcrumbs
½ cup pine nuts
¼ cup fresh parmesan cheese,
   finely grated
¼ cup chopped fresh basil or
   parsley
1 egg, lightly beaten

Sauce
1 tablespoon olive oil
1 onion, chopped
2 cloves garlic, crushed
425 g can tomatoes
2 tablespoons tomato paste
½ cup good quality white wine
1 teaspoon soft brown sugar
2 bay leaves

➤ PREHEAT OVEN to warm 160°C (315°F/Gas Mark 2–3).
1 Place chicken between two sheets plastic wrap. Using rolling pin or meat mallet, pound gently to flatten.
2 Combine breadcrumbs, pine nuts, parmesan and basil in bowl; mix well. Add egg, stir until all ingredients are moistened. Divide filling into 6 portions. Spread one portion evenly onto each fillet, roll fillets up, secure with toothpicks. Place seam-side down in single layer in ovenproof dish.
3 To make Sauce: Heat oil in medium pan. Add onion and garlic; cook over low heat 2–3 minutes or until just golden. Add tomatoes, tomato paste, wine, sugar and bay leaves and bring slowly to the boil. Reduce heat, simmer 6 minutes. Pour tomato sauce over chicken. Cover, bake 20–25 minutes or until chicken is cooked.

COOK'S FILE

Storage time: Dish can be made the day before it is required.
Hint: Veal escalopes can be used in place of chicken.

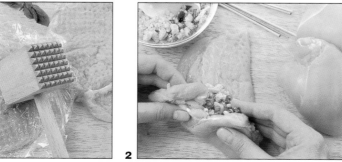

Coq au Vin (top) and
Chicken and Pine Nut Rolls in Tomato Sauce.

RABBIT BRAISED IN BEER

Preparation time: 40 minutes
Total cooking time: 2 hours 25 minutes
Serves 4–6

1 large rabbit (1.5 kg)
1/2 cup plain flour
salt and pepper
1/4 cup olive oil
2 medium onions, cut in thick
　　wedges
2 medium carrots, finely chopped
2 teaspoons soft brown sugar
1 cup beer
1/2 cup chicken stock or water
1/4 cup finely chopped parsley
2 teaspoons finely chopped
　　fresh thyme

1 teaspoon finely chopped fresh
　　rosemary
1 teaspoon finely chopped fresh
　　oregano
1 bay leaf
45 g butter
1 tablespoon flour, extra

➤ PREHEAT OVEN to moderate 180°C (350°F/Gas Mark 4). Cut rabbit into 8 portions. Combine flour, salt and pepper on baking paper. Toss meat in seasoned flour; shake off excess.

1 Heat oil in large heavy-based pan. Cook rabbit quickly in batches over medium heat until well browned; drain on paper towels. Add onion, cook 5 minutes or until just tender. Transfer to 8-cup capacity ovenproof dish. Add carrot, then rabbit pieces.

2 Heat sugar in pan. Add beer and stock or water. Bring to boil. Pour mixture over rabbit. Combine parsley, thyme, rosemary, oregano and bay leaf. Sprinkle half the herb mixture over rabbit. Cover, bake 2 hours or until tender.

3 Place butter in small bowl. Beat with wooden spoon until creamy. Gradually mix in flour until smooth. Add butter mixture to casserole in small amounts. Shake dish to mix through. Scatter remaining herbs over the top. Bake a further 5 minutes or until slightly thickened. Serve with steamed sliced zucchini and beans.

COOK'S FILE

Storage time: May be prepared up to step 3 and stored, covered, in refrigerator overnight. When required, reheat casserole; when hot, add butter and flour mixture, bake 5 minutes.

1

2

3

SPICY GARLIC CHICKEN

Preparation time: 30 minutes
Total cooking time: 1 hour
Serves 4–6

1.4 kg chicken
2 medium red onions
1 large red capsicum
1 small bunch coriander
2 tablespoons olive oil
4 cloves garlic, crushed
1 teaspoon ground ginger
1 teaspoon chilli powder
1 teaspoon caraway seeds,
    crushed
1 teaspoon ground turmeric
2 teaspoons ground coriander
2 teaspoons ground cumin
1¹/2 cups water
¹/2 cup raisins
¹/2 cup black olives
1 teaspoon finely grated
    lemon rind

➤ TRIM CHICKEN of excess fat and sinew. Cut chicken into 12 serving pieces.

1 Cut onions into thin rings. Remove seeds and membrane from capsicum. Cut into 1.5 cm squares. Finely chop coriander roots. Reserve coriander leaves for garnish.

2 Heat oil in large heavy-based pan. Add garlic, onion, capsicum, ginger, chilli, caraway, turmeric, coriander and cumin. Add coriander roots. Cook over medium heat 10 minutes.

3 Add chicken, stir until combined. Add water. Bring to boil, reduce heat. Simmer 45 minutes or until chicken is tender and cooked through.

4 Add raisins, olives and rind. Simmer a further 5 minutes. Serve with pasta or rice. May be served sprinkled with coriander leaves.

COOK'S FILE

Storage time: This dish is best eaten the day it is made.

Variations: Chicken pieces may be used instead of whole chicken. Use sultanas in place of raisins. Use chicken stock in place of water.

Hint: For extra flavour, heat 40 g butter in heavy-based frying pan. Cook chicken in small batches over medium-high heat or until well browned. Remove from pan and drain on paper towels. Add chicken to casserole as above.

FAMILY CHICKEN PIE

Preparation time: 40 minutes
Total cooking time: 1 hour
Serves 6

1 barbecued chicken

Pastry
2 cups self-raising flour
125 g butter, chopped
1 egg
2–3 tablespoons water

Filling
30 g butter
1 medium onion, finely
   chopped
310 g can creamed corn
1¼ cups cream

➤ REMOVE MEAT from chicken carcass; discard bones. Shred meat finely.
1 Process flour and butter in food processor until fine and crumbly. Add egg and almost all the liquid, process until mixture just comes together. Turn onto lightly floured surface. Knead until smooth. Cover with plastic wrap, refrigerate 20 minutes.
2 Preheat oven to moderate 180°C (350°F/Gas Mark 4). Heat butter in pan, add onion. Cook over medium heat 3 minutes. Add chicken, corn and cream. Bring to boil, reduce heat, simmer 10 minutes. Remove from heat, cool slightly.
3 Divide pastry in two. Roll half pastry, between two sheets of plastic wrap, large enough to cover base and sides of 23 cm pie dish. Spoon chicken mixture into pastry-lined dish.

4 Roll out remaining pastry large enough to cover top of pie. Brush with milk. Press edges together to seal. Trim edges with sharp knife. Roll remaining pastry into two long ropes, twist together. Brush pie edge with a little milk. Place pastry rope around rim of pie. Bake 45 minutes.

COOK'S FILE

Storage time: Cook this dish just before serving.

CHICKEN, LEEK AND WHITE WINE CASSEROLE

Preparation time: 30 minutes
Total cooking time: 1 hour
Serves 6

2 kg chicken thigh
   cutlets
1/2 cup plain flour
salt and pepper
2 tablespoons oil
30 g butter
4 bacon rashers, roughly
   chopped
2 medium leeks

2 celery sticks
2 cloves garlic, crushed
2 medium carrots, cut into thin
   strips
1 bay leaf
1 1/2 cups chicken stock
1 cup good quality white wine

➤ TRIM CHICKEN of excess fat and sinew.

1 Toss chicken pieces lightly in seasoned flour; shake off excess. Heat oil and butter in heavy-based pan. Cook chicken pieces quickly, in batches, until well browned. Drain on paper towels. Cook bacon 3 minutes until brown. Drain on paper towels. Drain excess fat from frying pan, leaving approximately 2 tablespoons.

2 Cut leek and celery into 5 cm-long strips, 1 cm-thick. Add to pan with garlic. Cook, stirring, until leek is soft.

3 Add chicken, bacon, carrots, bay leaf, stock and wine. Bring to boil, reduce heat and simmer, covered, 30 minutes. Remove lid, simmer 15 minutes until thickened slightly.

COOK'S FILE

Storage time: This dish can be cooked one day ahead and reheated. Store, covered, in refrigerator.
Hint: A whole large chicken can be jointed and used in this recipe.

CHICKEN AND HAM PIE

Preparation time: 40 minutes
Total cooking time: 1 hour
Makes one 20 cm pie

Pastry
3 cups plain flour
180 g butter, chopped
1/3 cup iced water

Filling
1 kg chicken mince
1/2 teaspoon dried thyme
1/2 teaspoon dried sage
2 eggs, lightly beaten
3 spring onions, finely chopped
2 teaspoons finely grated
   lemon rind
1 teaspoon French mustard
1/3 cup cream
100 g sliced leg ham, finely
   chopped
1 egg, lightly beaten, extra

➤ PREHEAT OVEN to moderate 180°C (350°F/Gas Mark 4). Place flour and butter in food processor.
1 Process for 20 seconds until mixture is fine and crumbly. Add almost all the water, process for 20 seconds or until mixture comes together. Turn onto a lightly floured surface, press together until smooth. Roll out two-thirds of the pastry and carefully line a 20 cm springform tin, bringing pastry up 2 cm higher than the sides. Cover with plastic wrap until required. Keep pastry trimmings for decoration.
2 To make Filling: Place chicken, herbs, eggs, onions, rind, mustard and cream in a large bowl and stir with a wooden spoon until well combined. Place half the chicken mixture into pastry-lined tin and smooth surface. Top with the chopped ham, then remaining chicken mixture.
3 Brush around inside edge of pastry with egg. Roll out the remaining pastry and lay over top of mixture. Press edges of pastry together. Trim pastry edges with a sharp knife.
4 Turn pastry edges down. Use index finger to make indentations around inside edge. Decorate top or leave plain. (See page 10 for decoration ideas.) Brush top of pie with beaten egg and bake for 1 hour or until golden brown. Serve pie warm or at room temperature.

COOK'S FILE

Storage time: Keep for up to two days in an airtight container in the refrigerator.
Hint: This pie is excellent for taking on a picnic. Cool pie completely, refrigerate in an airtight container overnight. When required, serve with a fresh green salad.

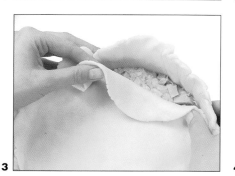

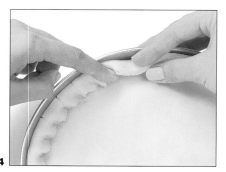

CHICKEN PAPRIKA

Preparation time: 25 minutes
Total cooking time: 45 minutes
Serves 4–6

800 g chicken thigh fillets
1/2 cup plain flour
salt and pepper
1 tablespoon oil
1 tablespoon oil, extra
2 medium onions, chopped
1–2 cloves garlic, crushed
2 tablespoons sweet paprika
1/2 cup good quality red wine
1 tablespoon tomato paste

425 g can tomatoes
200 g button mushrooms
1/2 cup chicken stock
2/3 cup sour cream

➤ RINSE CHICKEN and dry well.
1 Trim chicken of excess fat and sinew. Cut chicken into 3 cm pieces. Toss chicken pieces lightly in seasoned flour, shake off excess and reserve flour. Heat oil in large heavy-based pan. Cook chicken quickly in small batches over medium-high heat, drain on paper towels.

2 Heat extra oil in pan, add onion and garlic. Cook, stirring, until onion is soft. Add paprika and reserved flour, stir 1 minute. Add chicken, wine, paste and undrained crushed tomatoes. Bring to boil, reduce heat. Simmer, covered, 15 minutes.

3 Add mushrooms and stock, simmer, covered, a further 10 minutes. Add sour cream, stir until heated through; do not allow to boil.

COOK'S FILE

Storage time: This recipe is best made on day of serving. Can be made, up to the stage of adding sour cream, a day ahead. Stir in sour cream when food is warmed through, being careful not to boil as this may cause the sauce to curdle.

TURKEY POT ROAST

Preparation time: 20 minutes
Total cooking time: 1 hour 15 minutes
Serves 6

1 kg frozen turkey breast roll
2 tablespoons oil
20 g butter
1 medium onion, cut into
    wedges
¹/₂ cup chicken stock
¹/₂ cup white wine
300 g sweet potato, cut into
    3 cm pieces
2 medium zucchini, cut into
    2 cm slices
¹/₂ cup redcurrant jelly
1 tablespoon cornflour
1 tablespoon water

➤ PREHEAT OVEN to moderate
180°C (350°F/Gas Mark 4).

1 Thaw turkey according to label.
Remove elasticised string from turkey,
and tie up securely with string, at
regular intervals, to retain its shape.
Heat oil and butter in a frying pan;
add turkey and brown all over on a
high heat. Transfer turkey to an 8-cup
capacity casserole dish.

2 Place onion wedges around the
turkey; pour stock and wine over.
Cover the casserole dish and bake for
40 minutes. Add sweet potato to dish,
bake 10 minutes. Add zucchini and
bake for a further 20 minutes.

3 Transfer turkey and vegetables to
a plate and keep warm. Strain liquid
into a small pan; add redcurrant jelly
and stir to combine.

4 Combine cornflour and water in a

small jug, stir until smooth. Add
gradually to pan, stirring, until mixture boils and thickens. Slice turkey
and serve with vegetables and sauce.

COOK'S FILE

Storage time: Turkey can be
cooked a day in advance. Reheat
gently to serve, or serve cold.
Variation: Use green and yellow
baby squash in place of the zucchini.

CHICKEN POT PIES WITH HERB SCONES

Preparation time: 25 minutes
Total cooking time: 35 minutes
Serves 6

60 g butter
1 medium onion, chopped
1/3 cup plain flour
2 2/3 cups milk
1 cup grated cheddar cheese
2 teaspoons seeded mustard
2 1/2 cups chopped cooked chicken
2 cups frozen mixed vegetables

Topping
2 cups self-raising flour
15 g butter

1 cup milk
2 tablespoons chopped fresh parsley
1 tablespoon milk, extra

➤ PREHEAT OVEN to hot 210°C (415°F/Gas Mark 6–7). Lightly grease six 1-cup capacity individual dishes with oil or melted butter.

1 Heat butter in large heavy-based pan. Add onion, cook over medium heat until soft. Add flour, stir over heat 1 minute or until lightly golden and bubbling. Add milk gradually to pan, stirring constantly over heat until sauce boils and thickens. Remove from heat. Stir in cheese, mustard, chicken and vegetables. Spoon mixture evenly into prepared dishes.

2 To make Topping: Place flour in medium bowl. Using fingertips, rub butter into flour for 2 minutes, until mixture is fine and crumbly. Make a well in centre. Stir in milk and parsley with a flat-bladed knife. Using a cutting action, stir until mixture is soft and sticky. Turn onto floured surface.

3 Using floured hands, knead until just smooth. Pat with hand to 2.5 cm thickness. Cut rounds from pastry with 4.5 cm cutter. Re-roll pastry cuttings to cut more rounds. Place three rounds on top of each chicken pot. Brush top with extra milk. Bake for 25 minutes or until scones are browned and cooked and the chicken mixture heated through.

COOK'S FILE

Storage time: Cook chicken mixture a day ahead. Store, covered, in refrigerator. Prepare scones just before required.

1

2

3

CHICKEN AND SUGAR SNAP PEA PARCELS

Preparation time: 40 minutes
Total cooking time: 30 minutes
Makes 8

6 chicken thigh fillets (900 g)
200 g sugar snap peas
150 g feta cheese
1 tablespoon oil
40 g butter
2 tablespoons plain flour
3/4 cup chicken stock
2/3 cup dry white wine
1 tablespoon seeded mustard
1/3 cup sliced sun-dried tomatoes, finely chopped, optional
24 sheets filo pastry
60 g butter, extra, melted
sesame and sunflower seeds

➤ PREHEAT OVEN to hot 210°C (415°F/Gas Mark 6–7). Trim chicken of fat and sinew. Cut chicken into 1 cm thick strips. Top and tail the peas, plunge into boiling water 1 minute or until bright in colour but still crunchy, drain well. Cut feta into 1 cm cubes.

1 Heat oil in heavy-based pan, cook chicken quickly, in small batches, over medium heat until well browned. Drain on paper towels.

2 Melt butter in pan, add flour. Stir over low heat 2 minutes or until flour mixture is lightly golden and bubbling. Add stock, wine and mustard, stirring until mixture is smooth. Stir constantly over medium heat until mixture boils and thickens. Stir in chicken, sugar snap peas, feta and tomatoes, mix gently. Remove from heat; cool. Divide mixture evenly into eight portions.

3 Brush three sheets of pastry with butter. Lay sheets on top of each other. Place one portion of mixture at one short end of pastry. Roll and fold pastry, enclosing filling to form a parcel. Brush with a little more butter, place seam-side down on greased oven tray. Repeat with remaining pastry, butter and filling. Brush tops with butter. Sprinkle with sesame and sunflower seeds. Bake 20 minutes or until golden brown and heated through.

COOK'S FILE

Storage time: This dish is best cooked on same day as required for serving. Suitable for freezing.

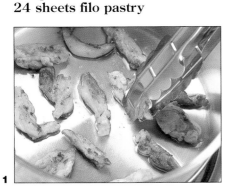

1

2

3

THAI COCONUT CHICKEN

Preparation time: 20 minutes
Total cooking time: 55 minutes
Serves 4

8 chicken thigh fillets
1/2 cup plain flour
1 tablespoon oil
1 tablespoon oil, extra
2 medium onions, chopped
2 teaspoons grated fresh ginger
1 clove garlic, crushed
1 teaspoon sambal oelek
1 1/2 cups coconut cream
1 tablespoon fish sauce

1 tablespoon turmeric
1 tablespoon soft brown sugar
2 tablespoons lime juice
1 tablespoon finely chopped
**   lemon grass**
1/4 cup chopped fresh coriander
4 spring onions, chopped

➤ PREHEAT OVEN to moderate 180°C (350°F/Gas Mark 4). Trim chicken of excess fat and sinew. Toss chicken in flour, shake off excess.
1 Heat oil in heavy-based pan. Cook chicken quickly, in small batches, over medium-high heat until well browned. Drain on paper towels.
2 Heat extra oil in pan. Add onions,

ginger, garlic, and sambal oelek, stir 1 minute or until fragrant. Add coconut cream, sauce, turmeric, sugar, juice and lemon grass, stir until heated through. Remove from heat.
3 Place chicken in large casserole dish. Pour sauce over chicken, bake in oven 45 minutes, or until chicken is tender. Serve sprinkled with chopped fresh coriander and spring onions.

COOK'S FILE

Storage time: This recipe is best made close to serving.
Hint: Use lemon juice in place of lime juice if preferred. Fresh lemon grass is available from the greengrocer.

DUCK WITH PEAS

Preparation time: 30 minutes
Total cooking time: 1 hour 40 minutes
Serves 4

2 kg duck
2 cups water
salt and black pepper
18 small new potatoes (700 g)
30 g butter
1/2 (250 g) iceberg lettuce,
**   coarsely shredded**
1 medium onion, chopped
2 cups fresh or frozen peas
1/4 cup parsley sprigs

1 teaspoon sugar
30 g butter, extra
1 tablespoon plain flour

➤ TRIM DUCK of excess fat. Cut in 10 portions. Preheat oven to moderate 180°C (350°F/Gas Mark 4).
1 Place duck in heavy-based frying pan. Cook in batches over low heat 4–5 minutes or until browned on all sides. (The fat will begin to run, discard any excess.) Transfer duck to a 10-cup capacity ovenproof dish. Discard any remaining fat in pan. Add water, salt and pepper. Stir over medium heat 2 minutes. Pour liquid over duck. Bake 45 minutes or until almost tender.

2 Peel potatoes. Halve if potatoes are large. Add to casserole. Bake further 10 minutes. Heat butter in pan. Add lettuce and onion. Cook over medium heat 3–4 minutes or until softened. Add peas, parsley and sugar. Stir until sugar dissolves. Add mixture to duck. Cook a further 30 minutes. Skim fat from surface of casserole.
3 Combine extra butter and flour. Add to casserole in small amounts, shake the dish well to distribute. Bake for another 5 minutes. Serve.

COOK'S FILE

Storage time: This recipe is best made close to serving time.

Thai Coconut Chicken (top) and
Duck with Peas.

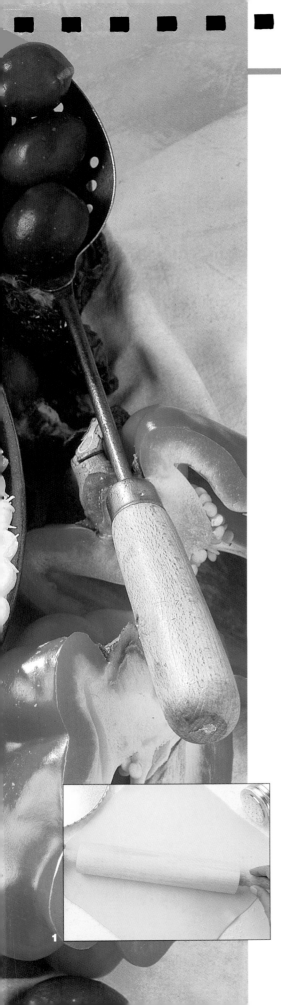

VEGETABLES

ROASTED CAPSICUM AND OLIVE PIE

Preparation time: 20 minutes
Total cooking time: 30 minutes
Serves 4–6

2 sheets ready-rolled shortcrust pastry
1 cup pitted black olives
1 teaspoon olive oil
2 cloves garlic, crushed
1/2 teaspoon sugar
1 medium red capsicum
1 yellow capsicum
1 tablespoon oil
1 large red onion, cut into thin wedges
2/3 cup finely grated gruyere cheese

➤ PREHEAT OVEN to hot 210°C (415°F/Gas Mark 6–7). Lightly grease a 23 cm round fluted flan tin with melted butter or oil.

1 Place one sheet of pastry on lightly floured surface. Brush with a little water, top with other pastry sheet. Roll pastry large enough to line prepared tin. Ease pastry into tin, trim edge with a sharp knife. Cut a sheet of baking paper large enough to cover pastry-lined tin. Spread a layer of dried beans or rice over the paper. Bake 10 minutes, remove paper and beans or rice, cook for a further 10 minutes or until lightly browned.

2 Place olives, oil, garlic and sugar in food processor bowl. Process until smooth. Spread mixture over base of prepared pastry case.

3 Cut capsicum into quarters. Place skin-side up on oven tray, grill until skin blisters and blackens. Cover with a damp tea-towel; cool slightly. Peel away skin; cut capsicum into 1 cm strips. Heat oil in small pan, add onion and cook over medium heat until soft. Add sliced capsicum, heat through. Sprinkle half the cheese over the olive mixture. Spoon capsicum and onion mixture over cheese. Top with remaining cheese, bake for 10 minutes or until cheese has melted and pie is heated through.

COOK'S FILE

Storage time: Pastry case can be cooked one day ahead and stored in airtight container. Olive paste and grilled capsicum can be prepared a day ahead and stored, covered, in the refrigerator. Assemble pie as close to serving time as possible.

Hints: If you grill capsicum until the skin blisters and blackens and then peel off the skin, you will find that when added to any dish the result is a much sweeter taste. If capsicum is not prepared in this way, it can cause the dish to taste bitter.

Red onions are milder and sweeter than other onions and are excellent for dishes like this one.

This pie makes a good lunch or light dinner. Serve with a fresh, crisp mixed salad tossed with your favourite dressing and sprinkled with chopped fresh coriander, parsley or other herbs.

ASPARAGUS STRUDEL

Preparation time: 20 minutes
Total cooking time: 35 minutes
Serves 4

2 bunches fresh asparagus
1 tablespoon oil
2 small onions, chopped
130 g can corn kernels, drained
1/4 cup chopped fresh parsley
2 tablespoons chopped fresh
  basil
2 tablespoons freshly grated
  parmesan cheese
2/3 cup grated cheddar cheese

1 egg
6 sheets filo pastry
40 g butter, melted
2 tablespoons grated fresh
  parmesan cheese, extra

➤ CUT ASPARAGUS into 3 cm lengths. Steam 1 minute. Preheat oven to hot 210°C (415°F/Gas Mark 6–7).
1 Heat oil in large heavy-based pan. Add onions. Cook, stirring, over medium heat for 3 minutes or until soft. Add asparagus, corn, parsley, basil, parmesan and cheddar cheese. Mix well; remove from heat, cool to room temperature. Add egg, stir well to combine.

2 Brush pastry sheets with melted butter. Layer sheets on top of each other. Place asparagus mixture along one long end of pastry. Form into log shape with hands. Roll pastry tightly, enclosing filling, folding in ends to form a parcel.
3 Place on greased oven tray. Brush with remaining butter, sprinkle with extra parmesan cheese. Bake for 25 minutes or until lightly browned and cooked through. Serve sliced as first course or main meal.

COOK'S FILE

Storage time: This recipe is best made on day of serving.

EGGPLANT AND POTATO BAKE

Preparation time: 25 minutes
Total cooking time: 1 hour 30 minutes
Serves 6

2 medium eggplant (570 g)
4 medium potatoes (550 g)
1/4 cup oil
1 tablespoon oil, extra
2 large onions, sliced
2 cloves garlic, crushed
2 x 425 g cans tomatoes
1/2 teaspoon sugar
1 1/2 cups grated cheddar cheese

➤ PREHEAT OVEN to hot 210°C (415°F/Gas Mark 6–7). Cut eggplant lengthways into 1 cm-thick slices. Spread out on tray, sprinkle generously with salt. Leave for 20 minutes. Wash, dry well with tea-towel. Peel potatoes, cut into very thin slices.

1 Heat oil in heavy-based pan and cook eggplant, in batches, until browned on both sides. Drain on paper towels.

2 Heat extra oil in same pan, add onion and cook over medium heat 4 minutes or until soft. Add garlic, undrained crushed tomatoes and sugar. Bring to boil, reduce heat. Simmer, uncovered, for 4 minutes, stirring occasionally.

3 Lightly grease a 12-cup capacity casserole dish. Place a layer of potato over base of dish, top with one-third of the cheese, half the eggplant and half the tomato sauce. Repeat layering, ending with tomato and cheese. Bake, covered with foil, for 1 hour 15 minutes or until potato is tender.

COOK'S FILE

Storage time: This dish can be cooked one day ahead and reheated.

INDIVIDUAL VEGETABLE POT PIES

Preparation time: 40 minutes
Total cooking time: 35 minutes
Makes 6

1 medium potato, peeled, cut into 1 cm cubes
150 g pumpkin, peeled, cut into 1 cm cubes
1 large carrot, peeled, cut into 1 cm cubes
150 g small broccoli florets
1 tablespoon oil
1 medium onion, finely chopped
1 medium red capsicum, cut into 1 cm squares
50 g butter
2 tablespoons plain flour
1 1/2 cups milk
1 cup grated cheddar cheese
2 egg yolks
salt and cayenne pepper to taste
2 sheets ready-rolled puff pastry
1 egg, lightly beaten
1 teaspoon poppy seeds

➤ PREHEAT OVEN to hot 210°C (415°F/Gas Mark 6–7). Brush six 1-cup capacity ramekins with oil.

1 Steam or microwave potato, pumpkin, carrot and broccoli until just tender. Drain well, place in large mixing bowl. Heat oil in frying pan, cook onion and capsicum over medium heat 2 minutes until soft. Add to bowl.

2 Heat butter in pan, add flour. Stir over low heat 2 minutes or until lightly golden. Add milk gradually to pan, stirring until mixture is smooth. Stir constantly over medium heat for 3 minutes or until mixture boils and thickens. Boil for another minute. Remove from heat, cool slightly. Add cheese and yolks to sauce, stir to combine. Season to taste.

3 Add sauce to vegetables; stir to combine. Divide mixture between prepared ramekins. Cut six circles from pastry to fit top of ramekins. Place on top of vegetable mixture. Press edges to seal. Brush with beaten egg and sprinkle with poppy seeds. Bake for 30 minutes, until golden brown.

COOK'S FILE

Storage time: These pies are best eaten the same day they are made.

1

2

3

SWEET VEGETABLE CURRY

Preparation time: 20 minutes
Total cooking time: 40 minutes
Serves 4

2 medium carrots
1 medium parsnip
1 medium potato
2 tablespoons oil
2 medium onions, chopped
1 teaspoon ground cardamom
$^1/_4$ teaspoon ground cloves
$1^1/_2$ teaspoons cumin seeds
1 teaspoon ground coriander
1 teaspoon turmeric
1 teaspoon brown mustard seeds
$^1/_2$ teaspoon chilli powder

2 teaspoons grated fresh ginger
$1^1/_3$ cups vegetable stock
$^3/_4$ cup apricot nectar
2 tablespoons fruit chutney
1 medium green capsicum, cut into 2 cm squares
200 g small button mushrooms
300 g cauliflower, cut into small florets
$^1/_4$ cup ground almonds

➤ CUT CARROTS, parsnip and potato into 2 cm pieces.
1 Heat oil in large heavy-based pan. Add onions, cook over medium heat 4 minutes or until just soft. Add cardamom, cloves, cumin seeds, coriander, turmeric, mustard seeds, chilli powder and grated ginger; cook, stirring, 1 minute or until aromatic.

2 Add carrots, parsnip, potato, stock, nectar and chutney. Cook, covered, over medium heat, stirring occasionally, for 25 minutes.
3 Stir in capsicum, mushrooms and cauliflower. Simmer 10 minutes more or until vegetables are tender. Stir in ground almonds. Serve.

COOK'S FILE

Storage time: This dish can be cooked one day ahead and reheated. Store, covered, in refrigerator.
Hints: Any vegetables may be used in this curry. For example, broccoli, zucchini, red capsicum or orange sweet potato would be suitable.
May be served with steamed rice.
Add one can of chickpeas to make this a complete meal.

LENTIL BHUJIA CASSEROLE

Preparation time: 40 minutes +
  overnight soaking
Total cooking time: 1 hour 10 minutes
Serves 4–6

2 cups green lentils
1 large onion, grated
1 large potato, grated
1 teaspoon ground cumin
1 teaspoon ground coriander
1 teaspoon ground turmeric
3/4 cup plain flour
oil for shallow frying
2 tablespoons oil, extra
2 cloves garlic, crushed
1 tablespoon grated ginger

1 cup tomato purée
2 cups vegetable stock
1 cup cream
200 g green beans
2 medium carrots, sliced
2 hard-boiled eggs, chopped
  (optional)

➤ SOAK LENTILS in cold water overnight. Drain well. Drain excess liquid from onion and potato.

1 Combine lentils, onion, potato, cumin, coriander, turmeric and flour in bowl. Mix well. Roll mixture into walnut-sized balls. Place on foil-lined tray. Cover, refrigerate 30 minutes.

2 Heat oil in heavy-based frying pan. Fry lentil balls in small batches over high heat for 5 minutes or until golden brown. Drain on paper towels.

3 Heat extra oil in heavy-based pan. Add garlic and ginger. Cook over medium heat 2 minutes or until golden. Stir in tomato purée, stock and cream. Bring to boil, reduce heat, simmer 10 minutes. Trim tops and tails of beans. Add to pan with lentil balls and carrots, cover, cook 30 minutes, stirring occasionally. Add egg, cook for 10 minutes. Serve with pitta bread.

COOK'S FILE

Storage time: The lentil balls may be made a day ahead and stored in an airtight container in the refrigerator.
Hint: Make sure your hands are dry when shaping mixture into balls.
Variation: Brown lentils or split peas are suitable for this recipe. They also need to be soaked.

1

2

3

CHEESE AND MUSHROOM PIES

Preparation time: 20 minutes
Total cooking time: 25 minutes
Makes 6

40 g butter
2 cloves garlic, crushed
500 g button mushrooms,
    sliced
1/2 large red capsicum, finely
    chopped
2/3 cup sour cream
3 teaspoons seeded mustard
1/2 cup finely grated gruyére or
    cheddar cheese
6 sheets ready-rolled puff
    pastry
1/2 cup finely grated gruyére or
    cheddar cheese, extra
1 egg, lightly beaten

➤ PREHEAT OVEN to hot 210°C (415°F/Gas Mark 6–7). Lightly grease two oven trays with melted butter.

1 Heat butter in large pan. Add garlic and mushrooms, cook over medium heat, stirring occasionally, until mushrooms are tender and liquid has evaporated. Remove from heat; cool. Stir in capsicum.

2 Combine sour cream, mustard and cheese in small bowl; mix well. Cut 12 circles with a 14 cm diameter from pastry. Spread cream mixture over six of the circles, leaving a 1 cm border. Top each with mushroom mixture.

3 Sprinkle each with two teaspoons of extra cheese. Brush around outer edges with beaten egg, place reserved pastry rounds on top of filling, sealing edges with a fork. Brush tops of the pastry with egg. Sprinkle remaining cheese over pastry. Place pies on oven trays, bake 20 minutes or until lightly browned and puffed.

COOK'S FILE

Storage time: This recipe is best made on day of serving.

Hint: Freshly grated parmesan or pecorino cheese may be substituted in this recipe.

1

2

3

LAYERED POTATO AND APPLE BAKE

Preparation time: 20 minutes
Total cooking time: 45 minutes
Serves 6

2 large potatoes
3 medium green apples
1 medium onion
¹/₂ cup finely grated cheddar
cheese
1 cup cream
¹/₄ teaspoon ground nutmeg
black pepper

➤ PREHEAT OVEN to moderate 180°C (350°F/Gas Mark 4). Brush a shallow 2-litre ovenproof dish with melted butter or oil.

1 Peel potatoes and cut into 5 mm slices. Peel, core and quarter apples. Cut into 5 mm slices. Slice onion into very fine rings.

2 Layer potatoes, apple and onions into prepared dish, ending with a layer of potato. Sprinkle evenly with cheese. Pour cream over top, covering as evenly as possible.

3 Sprinkle with nutmeg and freshly ground black pepper to taste. Bake for 45 minutes, until golden brown.

Remove from oven and set aside for 5 minutes before serving.

Note: To prevent the sliced potato and apple browning before assembling dish, place in a bowl of cold water with a squeeze of lemon juice. Drain and pat dry with paper towels before using.

COOK'S FILE

Storage time: Can be made up to a day ahead.

Hint: This dish is good with pork and chicken. If you prefer to make it a complete meal, add 150 g finely sliced leg ham to layers.

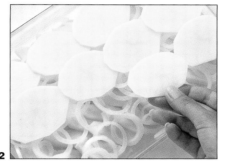

SPICY CHICKPEA AND VEGETABLE CASSEROLE

Preparation time: 25 minutes + overnight soaking
Total cooking time: 1 hour 30 minutes
Serves 4

1 ¹/₂ cups dried chickpeas
2 tablespoons oil
1 large onion, chopped
1 clove garlic, crushed
3 teaspoons ground cumin
¹/₂ teaspoon chilli powder
¹/₂ teaspoon allspice
425 g can peeled tomatoes,
crushed
1 ¹/₂ cups vegetable stock

300 g pumpkin, cut into 2 cm
cubes
150 g green beans, topped
and tailed
200 g button squash, quartered
2 tablespoons tomato paste
1 teaspoon dried oregano

➤ PLACE CHICKPEAS in a large bowl, cover with cold water and soak overnight; drain.

1 Heat oil in a large pan, add onion and garlic; stir-fry for 2 minutes or until tender. Add cumin, chilli and all-spice and stir-fry 1 minute.

2 Add chickpeas, tomatoes and stock to pan. Bring to boil, reduce heat and simmer, covered, for 1 hour, stirring occasionally.

3 Add pumpkin, beans, squash, tomato paste and oregano. Stir to combine. Simmer, covered, for a further 15 minutes. Remove lid from pan and simmer uncovered for a further 10 minutes to reduce and thicken sauce slightly.

COOK'S FILE

Storage time: Will keep for up to three days in an airtight container in the refrigerator.

Hint: A quick way to soak chickpeas is to place them in a large saucepan and cover with cold water. Bring to the boil, remove from heat and soak for two hours. If you are in a hurry, substitute with canned chickpeas. Drain and rinse thoroughly before use.

Layered Potato and Apple Bake (top)
and Spicy Chickpea and Vegetable Casserole.

POTATO PIE

Preparation time: 35 minutes
Total cooking time: 1 hour +
  10 minutes standing
Serves 6

Pastry
2 1/2 cups plain flour
150 g butter, chopped
2–3 tablespoons iced water

Filling
3 medium potatoes, peeled
30 g butter
3 medium onions, thinly sliced
2/3 cup chopped fresh parsley
1 1/2 cups grated cheddar cheese
1 teaspoon cracked black pepper
60 g butter, extra, melted
1 egg, lightly beaten
1 cup cream

➤ BRUSH a 23 cm round pie plate with melted butter or oil.

1 Place flour in food processor; add butter. Process 30 seconds or until mixture is fine and crumbly. Add almost all the liquid, process 20 seconds or until mixture comes together. Turn mixture onto lightly floured surface. Knead gently 1–2 minutes or until smooth. Cover with plastic wrap, refrigerate 15 minutes.

2 Cut potato into thin slices. Heat butter in large pan. Add onions, cook over low heat 15–20 minutes or until very soft. Cool slightly.

3 Preheat oven to hot 210°C (415°F/ Gas Mark 6–7). Roll two-thirds of pastry between two sheets of baking paper, large enough to cover base and sides of prepared dish. Layer potato slices, onions, parsley, cheese and pepper alternately until all ingredients are used. Press down firmly after each layer. Pour butter over. Brush pastry edges with egg. Roll remaining pastry large enough to cover pie top. Place pastry over pie. Press edges together to seal. Re-roll pastry trimmings. Cut out leaf shapes. Trim edges. Brush pie top with egg.

4 Place leaf shapes around edge of pie, brush with egg. Cut small holes in the centre of pie to release the steam. Bake 1 hour. Check pie after 45 minutes to ensure pastry is not burnt. Cover with foil to prevent further browning. Remove from oven. Bring cream to boil in pan, reduce heat, simmer until reduced by one-third. Pour hot cream in pie steam holes. Allow to stand 10 minutes. Cut into wedges.

COOK'S FILE

Storage time: This pie is best eaten just after baking.
Hint: Use ready-rolled shortcrust pastry in the recipe if preferred.

MEXICAN TOMATO CASSEROLE

Preparation time: 25 minutes
Total cooking time: 20 minutes
Serves 4–6

2 tablespoons oil
2 red onions, chopped
2 cloves garlic, crushed
6 medium ripe tomatoes, peeled, seeded and chopped
1 medium green capsicum, seeded and chopped
1 tablespoon red wine vinegar
1 teaspoon sugar

$^{1}/_{2}$ teaspoon ground chilli powder
375 g can corn kernels, drained
125 g packet plain corn chips
1 $^{1}/_{4}$ cups (125 g) grated cheddar cheese
1 cup sour cream
$^{1}/_{2}$ cup chopped chives

➤ PREHEAT OVEN to warm 160°C (315°F/Gas Mark 2–3).

1 Heat oil in medium heavy-based pan. Add onions and garlic, cook over medium heat for 3 minutes. Add tomatoes, capsicum, vinegar, sugar and chilli powder. Cook uncovered 6–7 minutes or until tomatoes are soft and most of the liquid has evaporated.

Add corn kernels; stir over low heat for 3 minutes.

2 Arrange layers of corn chips, sauce and cheese in a casserole dish, finishing with cheese layer.

3 Spread sour cream evenly on top. Bake uncovered for 15 minutes. Sprinkle with chives before serving.

COOK'S FILE

Storage time: Recipe is best eaten within one hour of making.
Variations: Use cheese or chilli-flavoured corn chips.
More chilli powder may be added for a spicier taste.
Hint: Serve with guacamole.

1

2

3

1

2

3

4

EGGPLANT AND TOMATO BAKE

Preparation time: 20 minutes
Total cooking time: 1 hour
   15 minutes
Serves 6

2 large eggplant
¹/₄ cup olive oil
2 large onions, chopped
1 teaspoon ground cumin
1 cup good quality white wine
800 g can tomatoes, crushed
2 cloves garlic, crushed
2 red chillies, finely chopped,
   optional
¹/₂ cup currants
¹/₄ cup chopped fresh coriander

➤ PREHEAT OVEN to hot 210°C (415°F/Gas Mark 6–7). Cut eggplant in 2 cm-thick rounds. Place on tray, sprinkle generously with salt. Leave for 20 minutes.

1 Heat 2 tablespoons oil in large pan. Add onions, cook over medium heat 5 minutes or until softened. Add cumin, stir 1 minute. Add wine. Bring to boil, reduce heat, simmer for 10 minutes or until mixture has reduced by three-quarters.

2 Add tomatoes. Bring to boil, reduce heat, cook 10 minutes. Add garlic, chillies and currants. Simmer further 5 minutes. Remove from heat.

3 Rinse eggplant. Squeeze dry in clean paper towels. Heat remaining oil in large frying pan. Fry eggplant slices over medium heat 3–4 minutes or until golden. Drain on paper towels.

4 Layer eggplant and tomato mixture in an 8-cup capacity casserole dish, sprinkle coriander between each layer. Finish with eggplant layer. Bake for 30 minutes. Serve with pasta and fresh sprigs of thyme.

COOK'S FILE

Storage time: Tomato mixture can be prepared several hours in advance. Assemble casserole just before it is to be baked.

PASTA AND VEGETABLES

Preparation time: 20 minutes
Total cooking time: 40–45 minutes
Serves 4

1 tablespoon olive oil
1 large onion, finely chopped
1 clove garlic, crushed
3 medium zucchini, sliced
4 button mushrooms, sliced
2 cups tomato pasta sauce
1 cup frozen peas
salt and pepper to taste
1 tablespoon oil, extra

1 1/2 cups dried pasta (penne or
   spiralli)
1/3 cup grated parmesan cheese

➤ PREHEAT OVEN to slow 150°C
(300°F/Gas Mark 2).

1 Heat oil in frying pan. Add onion
and garlic, cook over low heat for
4 minutes or until onion is soft. Add
zucchini and mushrooms, cook 3 minutes. Add sauce and peas, cook 3 minutes. Season to taste. Remove from
heat and set aside.

2 To a large pan of boiling water,
add oil and pasta, cook 10–12 minutes
or until tender. Drain, add to vegetables.

3 Spoon mixture into a casserole
dish. Sprinkle with parmesan and
bake, covered, for 20–30 minutes.

COOK'S FILE

Storage time: Can be made one day
before required.
Hint: If oil is added to the water
when cooking pasta, it will prevent
the pasta from sticking together.
Variations: Chopped fresh or dried
herbs such as parsley, basil or
oregano can be added to this dish.
You can vary the combination of
vegetables according to your own
taste and what is in season.

1

2

3

VEGETABLE PASTIES WITH RICH TOMATO SAUCE

Preparation time: 25 minutes
Total cooking time: 50 minutes
Makes 12

1 medium potato
1 medium carrot
1 medium parsnip
100 g pumpkin
2 teaspoons oil
1 medium onion, finely chopped
1/2 cup vegetable stock
1/3 cup fresh or frozen peas
1 tablespoon finely chopped
  fresh parsley
3 sheets ready-rolled puff pastry
1 egg, lightly beaten

Tomato Sauce
1 tablespoon oil
1 small onion, chopped
1 clove garlic, crushed
2 medium tomatoes, peeled and
  chopped
1/4 cup good quality red wine
1/4 cup vegetable stock
2 tablespoons tomato paste
1/2 teaspoon dried basil
1/2 teaspoon dried oregano

➤ PREHEAT OVEN to hot 210°C (415°F/Gas Mark 6–7). Brush an oven tray with melted butter or oil. Peel and cut potato, carrot, parsnip and pumpkin into 1 cm cubes.

1 Heat oil in a frying pan and cook onion over medium heat for 2 minutes or until soft. Add potato, carrot, parsnip, pumpkin and stock; bring to boil. Reduce heat and simmer for 10 minutes, stirring occasionally, until vegetables are soft and liquid has evaporated. Stir in peas and parsley and set aside to cool.

2 Using a plate as a guide, cut four 12 cm circles from each sheet of pastry. Place one level tablespoon of mixture onto each round, brush edges with water and bring up to meet in the centre above filling. Twist decoratively to seal. Brush with beaten egg, place on prepared tray and bake for 25 minutes until puffed and golden.

3 To make Tomato Sauce: Heat oil in a small pan, add onion and garlic and cook over medium heat 2 minutes or until soft. Add tomatoes, wine and stock; bring to the boil. Reduce heat, simmer for 15 minutes,

stirring occasionally. Remove from heat and cool. Place tomato mixture in food processor bowl. Process until smooth. Return mixture to pan, add tomato paste, basil and oregano, stir until hot. Serve hot or cold.

COOK'S FILE

Storage time: These pasties are best eaten the day they are made.
Hint: To peel tomatoes, mark a small cross on the top, place in boiling water for 1–2 minutes and then put immediately into cold water. Remove and peel skin down from the cross.

1

2

3

SILVERBEET PIE

Preparation time: 40 minutes
Total cooking time: 45 minutes
Serves 6–8

Pastry
2 cups plain flour
1/2 cup wholemeal plain flour
120 g butter, chopped
1/3–1/2 cup iced water

Filling
1 large bunch (about 800 g)
    silverbeet (chard)
1/2 cup chopped pistachio nuts
1/4 cup chopped raisins
1/3 cup grated parmesan cheese
1/2 cup grated cheddar cheese

3 eggs
2/3 cup cream
1/4 teaspoon ground nutmeg
1 egg, extra, beaten

➤ SIFT FLOURS into large mixing bowl; add chopped butter.

1 Using fingertips, rub butter into flour for 2 minutes or until mixture is fine and crumbly. Add almost all the liquid, mix to a firm dough, adding more liquid if necessary. Turn onto a lightly floured surface, press together until smooth. Roll out two-thirds of pastry and line a greased 23 cm pie dish. Wrap remaining pastry in plastic and refrigerate both for 20 minutes.

2 Preheat oven to moderate 180°C (350°F/Gas Mark 4). Remove stems from silverbeet and wash leaves.

Shred finely. Steam or microwave 3 minutes or until tender. Cool, squeeze to remove excess moisture; spread out to separate strands. Spread pistachios onto pastry base. Combine silverbeet, raisins and cheeses. Place over nuts. Whisk eggs, cream and nutmeg together, pour over silverbeet mixture.

3 Roll out remaining pastry large enough to cover top of pie. Place pastry over pie, trim edges with sharp knife. Press edges together to seal. Brush with beaten egg and decorate with pastry trimmings. Bake 45 minutes, until golden. Serve warm, with a tomato salad.

COOK'S FILE

Storage time: This pie is best eaten on the day it is made.

1

2

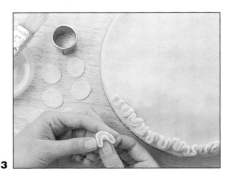

3

RICE AND RATATOUILLE WITH CHEESE CRUST

Preparation time: 45 minutes
Total cooking time: 55–60 minutes
Serves 4–6

2 large eggplant (500 g)
1 teaspoon salt
750 g tomatoes
1/3 cup olive oil
6 cloves garlic, peeled, chopped
2 large onions, cut in 2 cm cubes
salt and pepper to taste
2 large red capsicum, cut in 3 cm cubes
1 large green capsicum, cut in 3 cm cubes
2 zucchini (500 g), cut in 2 cm slices
1 teaspoon sugar
1 cup water
1 cup tomato juice
1/2 cup long grain rice

Topping
3 eggs
1/2 cup cream
2 teaspoons French mustard
1 cup grated cheddar cheese
salt and pepper

➤ PREHEAT OVEN to moderate 180°C (350°F/Gas Mark 4). Peel egg plant, cut into 3 cm cubes. Place into a colander. Sprinkle well with salt. Set aside 15 minutes. Rinse under cold water; drain. Dry with paper towels.

1 Mark a small cross on top of tomatoes. Place in boiling water 1–2 minutes and then immediately into cold water. Remove and peel down skin from cross. Cut tomatoes in quarters.

2 Heat oil in large heavy-based pan. Add eggplant, garlic and onion, cook over medium heat 5 minutes. Season with salt and pepper. Add capsicum, zucchini, tomatoes and sugar, cook a further 5 minutes. Remove from heat.

3 Add water, juice and rice, mix well. Transfer mixture to 8-cup capacity ovenproof dish. Cover. Bake 20–30 minutes or until rice has absorbed the liquid and is tender.

4 Whisk eggs, cream and mustard in large jug. Stir in cheese, season with salt and pepper. Pour mixture over cooked vegetables and rice. Bake 15 minutes or until mixture is set. Leave casserole to stand for 5 minutes before serving.

COOK'S FILE

Storage time: Serve immediately.
Hint: For a more subtle eggplant flavour, peel eggplant, cut into 3 cm cubes, place in pan, cover with water. Season. Cook 5 minutes or until tender. Drain. Reserve liquid. Use one cup to replace the water in this recipe.

SEAFOOD

HERBED FISH TARTLETS

Preparation time: 40 minutes
Total cooking time: 45 minutes
Makes 8

1 ¼ cups plain flour
90 g butter, chopped
1 tablespoon chopped fresh
    thyme
1 tablespoon chopped fresh dill
2 tablespoons chopped fresh
    parsley
¾ cup finely grated cheddar
    cheese
3–4 tablespoons iced water

Filling
400 g boneless white fish fillets
2 spring onions, finely chopped
2 tablespoons chopped fresh
    parsley
½ cup finely grated cheddar
    cheese
2 eggs
½ cup cream

➤ LIGHTLY GREASE eight 10 cm round fluted flan tins with melted butter or oil.

1 Sift flour into large mixing bowl, add chopped butter. Using fingertips, rub butter into flour for 2 minutes or until fine and crumbly. Stir in thyme, dill, parsley and cheese. Add almost all the water, mix to a firm dough, adding more water if necessary. Turn onto lightly floured surface. Knead dough gently until smooth. Cover pastry with plastic wrap and refrigerate for 15 minutes.

2 Preheat oven to hot 210°C (415°F/ Gas Mark 6–7). Divide pastry into eight portions. Roll each portion on lightly floured surface, large enough to fit prepared tins. Ease pastry into tins, trim edges with a sharp knife or rolling pin. Cover each pastry-lined tin with a sheet of greaseproof paper. Spread a layer of dried beans or rice evenly over paper. Bake for 10 minutes. Remove from oven; discard paper and beans or rice. Return to oven for a further 10 minutes or until lightly browned; cool.

3 Place fish in frying pan, add water to just cover. Bring to boil, reduce heat and simmer gently for 3 minutes. Remove from pan, drain. Allow to cool. Flake with a fork. Divide between cases, sprinkle with spring onions, parsley and cheese. In a jug, whisk together eggs and cream. Pour over fish mixture. Bake 25 minutes or until set and golden brown.

COOK'S FILE

Storage time: Cook this recipe just before serving.
Hint: Smoked fish may be used for this recipe. Serve with steamed potatoes and a salad.
Variation: If preferred, this recipe can be made in one 23 cm flan. Prepare ingredients as per instructions and place in greased flan tin. Cooking time may be a little longer but check after 25 minutes to see if flan is set.

SEAFOOD PARCELS

Preparation time: 25 minutes
Total cooking time: 35 minutes
Serves 4

250 g boneless white fish fillets
100 g scallops
30 g butter
1 tablespoon lemon juice
1 tablespoon plain flour
1 cup milk
1/2 cup grated cheddar cheese
1 tablespoon chopped fresh chives
1 tablespoon chopped fresh dill
200 g peeled, cooked prawns
10 sheets filo pastry
60 g butter, melted
2 teaspoons poppy seeds

➤ PREHEAT OVEN to moderate 180°C (350°F/Gas Mark 4). Line an oven tray with baking paper. Cut fish into 1 cm-wide strips. Wash scallops, remove brown vein, leaving corals intact.

1 Heat butter in heavy-based pan. Add fish, scallops and lemon juice. Cook over medium heat for 1 minute or until tender. Remove from pan with slotted spoon and keep warm.

2 Stir in flour. Add milk gradually to pan, stirring constantly over medium heat for 3 minutes or until mixture boils and thickens. Boil for another minute. Stir in cheese, chives, dill, fish, scallops and prawns. Remove from heat. Cover surface with plastic wrap.

3 Place two sheets of pastry on work surface. Brush each sheet with melted butter. Place one sheet of pastry on top of the other. Cut pastry in four equal strips using a sharp knife or scissors. Place two tablespoons of mixture on one short end of each pastry strip. Fold in edges and roll up. Repeat with remaining pastry and mixture. Place seam-side down on prepared tray. Brush with butter, sprinkle with poppy seeds. Bake for 20 minutes.

COOK'S FILE

Storage time: Sauce for this recipe may be made a day ahead. Cover with plastic wrap and refrigerate.

Hint: When using filo pastry, cover unused sheets with a damp tea-towel to prevent drying out.

Variations: Any seafood may be used in this recipe – try salmon fillets. Use sesame seeds to replace poppy seeds on top of pastry.

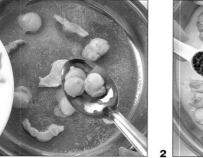

1

2

3

FISH AND MACARONI CASSEROLE

Preparation time: 20 minutes
Total cooking time: 50 minutes
Serves 4

1 cup macaroni
30 g butter
1 medium onion, chopped
500 g white fish fillets, cut into
    2 cm cubes
1 tablespoon chopped fresh
    thyme
100 g button mushrooms, sliced
1/2 teaspoon hot English mustard
1 tablespoon plain flour
1 cup chicken stock
1/2 cup cream
1/2 cup sour cream
1 cup fresh breadcrumbs
1 cup grated cheddar cheese
1/2 cup grated parmesan cheese
2 tablespoons chopped parsley

➤ PREHEAT OVEN to moderate 180°C (350°F/Gas Mark 4).

1 Cook macaroni in a large pan of rapidly boiling water with a little oil added until just tender. Drain and set aside.

2 Heat butter in a heavy-based pan. Add onion and cook over medium heat for 3 minutes or until golden. Add fish, thyme and mushrooms. Cook for 5 minutes or until fish is tender. Remove from pan. Keep warm.

3 Stir in mustard and flour. Add stock and cream gradually to pan. Stir constantly over medium heat for 3 minutes or until mixture boils and thickens; boil for another minute. Remove from heat, stir in sour cream. Transfer mixture to a large bowl; stir in macaroni, fish and mushrooms. Place into a large ovenproof dish. Combine breadcrumbs, cheeses and parsley. Sprinkle over macaroni mixture. Bake for 30 minutes or until golden. Serve with fresh green salad tossed with your favourite dressing.

COOK'S FILE

Storage time: Macaroni may be cooked a day ahead, tossed in a little oil to prevent it sticking together and stored in an airtight container in the refrigerator.

Hint: Any firm-fleshed white fish may be used in this recipe. If you prefer, you can use canned tuna. Drain the tuna before adding to recipe.

1

2

3

SEAFOOD PEPPERPOT

Preparation time: 20 minutes
Total cooking time: 55 minutes
Serves 6

500 g boneless white fish fillets
250 g medium green prawns
250 g mussels
200 g scallops
2 tablespoons oil
2 cloves garlic, crushed
2 large red onions, each cut
   into 8 wedges
1 large red capsicum, cut into
   thin strips
1 large green capsicum, cut into
   thin strips
3 small red chillies, seeded,
   chopped
850 g can peeled tomatoes,
   chopped
1 1/2 cups fish stock
1/4 cup chopped fresh basil

➤ CUT FISH into 2 cm cubes.
1 Peel and devein prawns, leaving tails intact. Scrub mussels; remove beard. Wash scallops; remove brown vein, leaving corals intact.
2 Heat oil in heavy-based pan. Add garlic and onion; cook over medium heat for 1 minute. Add capsicum and chilli. Cook for further 4 minutes. Stir in tomatoes, stock and basil. Bring to boil, reduce heat, cover and simmer 30 minutes.
3 Add prawns, fish and mussels, cook for 5 minutes, stirring occasionally. Add scallops; cook for 5 minutes or until tender. May be served with rice and crusty bread.

COOK'S FILE

Storage time: Make tomato sauce two days ahead. Store in refrigerator. Add basil when reheating.
Variation: Any firm-fleshed fish may be used in this recipe; calamari may be used instead of scallops.

TUNA MORNAY CASSEROLE

Preparation time: 15 minutes
Total cooking time: 30 minutes
Serves 4–6

40 g butter
2 spring onions, finely chopped
2 tablespoons plain flour
1 1/2 cups milk
3/4 cup grated cheddar cheese
2 x 425 g cans tuna, drained
1/4 cup fresh breadcrumbs
1/4 cup grated cheddar cheese,
   extra
2 tablespoons finely chopped
   parsley

➤ PREHEAT OVEN to hot 210°C (415°F/Gas Mark 6–7).
1 Heat butter in a medium pan; add spring onions and cook over low heat 2 minutes until soft. Add flour, stir over low heat 2 minutes, until mixture is lightly golden.
2 Add milk gradually to pan, stirring until mixture is smooth. Stir constantly over medium heat 4 minutes or until mixture boils and thickens; boil for another minute, remove from heat. Cool slightly, stir in grated cheese.
3 Add tuna to pan and fold through gently, taking care not to break up pieces too much. Transfer mixture to 5-cup capacity casserole dish. Sprinkle with combined breadcrumbs, extra cheese and parsley. Bake 20 minutes, or until golden brown. Serve immediately with rice or noodles, steamed vegetables or green salad.

COOK'S FILE

Storage time: This recipe is best made just before serving.
Hints: Salmon or any cooked fish or seafood may be used to replace tuna. Breadcrumbs can be replaced with cornflake crumbs or crushed cracker biscuits for an even crunchier topping.

*Seafood Pepperpot (top) and
Tuna Mornay.*

SEAFOOD MORNAY CASSEROLE

Preparation time: 25 minutes
Total cooking time: 40 minutes
Serves 4–6

3 medium white fish fillets
250 g medium green prawns
200 g scallops
400 g mussels
1 small onion, cut in half
2 bay leaves
1/2 lemon, sliced
1/2 cup good quality white wine

Sauce
45 g butter
1 stick celery, chopped
1 large carrot, finely chopped
6 teaspoons plain flour
1 1/2 cups milk
125 g gruyère cheese, grated
1 cup frozen peas

Topping
1 cup fresh white breadcrumbs
1/2 cup flaked almonds
2 teaspoons finely grated lemon rind
1/2 teaspoon freshly ground black pepper
60 g butter, chopped

➤ PREHEAT OVEN to moderate 180°C (350°F/Gas Mark 4).

1 Remove skin and bones from fish fillets; cut fish into 3 cm cubes. Peel and devein prawns. Wash scallops, remove brown vein. Remove beards from mussels and wash away any grit. Prise open shells, remove mussels; discard shells. Place fish, prawns, scallops and mussels in pan. Cover with cold water; add onion, bay leaves, lemon and wine. Bring slowly to the boil. Cover; reduce to low and simmer for 3–4 minutes. Remove seafood from cooking liquid. Place in lightly greased casserole dish.

2 To make Sauce: Heat butter in medium pan; add celery and carrot. Cook for 1 minute; add flour. Stir over low heat 2 minutes or until flour mixture is lightly golden. Add the milk gradually to pan, stirring until mixture is smooth. Stir constantly over medium heat for 3 minutes or until mixture boils and thickens; boil for another minute; remove from heat. Cool to room temperature.

3 Stir in cheese and peas. Pour sauce over seafood; mix gently to combine. **To make Topping:** Combine breadcrumbs, almonds, lemon rind and pepper in bowl. Mix well. Spread evenly over top of seafood mixture. Dot with butter. Bake for 20 minutes or until heated through and top is golden brown. Serve garnished with a sprig of dill if liked.

COOK'S FILE

Storage time: Mornay is best eaten on the day of preparation.
Hint: Any combination of cooked seafood can be used in this recipe. The cooking liquid can replace half the milk if desired.
Chopped fresh herbs, especially dill, chives and parsley, can be added to the sauce at the end of cooking time.

SEAFOOD STEW

Preparation time: 20 minutes
Total cooking time: 45 minutes
Serves 4–6

300 g medium green prawns
1/4 cup olive oil
2 medium onions, finely chopped
2 medium carrots, chopped
2 sticks celery, finely chopped
2 cloves garlic, crushed
6 medium tomatoes (1 kg),
    peeled and chopped
1/4 cup good quality white wine
2 tablespoons tomato paste
1 kg boneless fish fillets, cut
    into 3 cm pieces
salt and pepper
12 mussels, beards removed
1/4 cup good quality white wine,
    extra
2 tablespoons chopped parsley
1 tablespoon fresh thyme leaves

➤ PEEL AND DEVEIN prawns,
leaving tails intact.

1 Heat oil in pan. Cook onions
10 minutes. Add carrots, celery and
garlic. Cook, stirring, 10 minutes.

2 Add tomatoes and wine. Bring to
boil, reduce heat, simmer covered
20 minutes. Stir in tomato paste. Add
prawns. Cover, simmer 3 minutes.
Add fish, salt and pepper, simmer
2 minutes.

3 Place mussels in a large pan, add
extra wine. Cover, cook over medium
heat 2–3 minutes until mussels open.
Strain liquid from mussels into
tomato mixture, stir to combine.
Arrange mussels on top. Sprinkle
with parsley and thyme. Serve
immediately with crusty bread.

COOK'S FILE

Storage time: Serve immediately.

1

2

3

SALMON AND RICE PIE

Preparation time: 40 minutes
Total cooking time: 1 hour
Serves 8

3/4 **cup fish stock**
1/4 **cup white short grain rice**
40 g **butter**
2 **tablespoons plain flour**
2/3 **cup milk**
1 **egg, lightly beaten**
1/2 **cup fresh or frozen peas**
1/4 **cup finely chopped parsley**
2 **sheets ready-rolled puff**
pastry
2 x 200 g **cans pink salmon,**
drained
4 **hard-boiled eggs, quartered**
1 **egg, extra, lightly beaten**

➤ PREHEAT OVEN to hot 210°C (415°F/Gas Mark 6–7). Line two oven trays with baking paper.

1 Place stock in medium heavy-based pan. Bring to boil. Add rice, reduce heat. Simmer, covered, 10 minutes or until rice has absorbed all liquid. Remove from heat.

2 Heat butter in medium pan; add flour. Stir over low heat 2 minutes or until flour mixture is lightly golden. Add milk gradually to pan, stirring until mixture is smooth. Stir constantly over medium heat 5 minutes or until mixture boils and thickens; boil for 1 minute; remove from heat.

3 Cool slightly, stir in egg, peas and parsley. Carefully lay pastry sheets on work surface.

4 Place salmon in bowl, flake with a fork. Place salmon evenly in an oblong shape in the centre of each pastry sheet, leaving a 3 cm gap on two sides. Place quarters of eggs on top. Combine rice and pea mixture in medium mixing bowl. Mix well.

5 Spoon rice mixture evenly over salmon. Brush pastry edges with extra egg. Fold in pastry edges like a parcel. Turn over and place on tray seam-side down.

6 Make three diagonal slits in the top of each pie. Brush with egg. Bake for 30 minutes or until pastry is puffed and golden. Cut each pie into four to serve. Serve with fresh green salad.

COOK'S FILE

Storage time: May be served either hot or cold. Can be made several hours in advance. Reheat before serving.

Hint: Fish stock is made by combining fish trimmings in lightly salted water with your choice of vegetables and herbs. Bring to the boil. Using a spoon, remove any scum that forms on top of stock. Simmer for about 15 minutes. Wine may then be added and the mixture simmered for a further 15 minutes. The quantities will vary according to the dish for which it is required. As a guide, use one litre of salted water, a chopped carrot, a stick of celery and a medium onion. The heads and bones of the fish are added, the gills discarded. After the initial simmering, add a little red or white wine, if desired, and continue simmering. Add herbs like bay leaves and parsley, depending on the recipe for which the stock is to be used and your personal taste. If using fresh herbs, add towards the end of cooking. Choose herbs that do not have an overpowering flavour. Strong fresh herbs often result in a bitter flavour after being simmered for long periods. When cooked, strain the stock through a fine sieve into a bowl.

Variations: Add one to two tablespoons finely chopped gherkins to the rice mixture if desired.

Use red salmon or tuna in this recipe if preferred.

1

3

1

2

3

SMOKED COD FLAN

Preparation time: 30 minutes
Total cooking time: 55 minutes
Serves 6

Pastry
1 cup plain flour
60 g butter, chopped
1 egg
1 tablespoon lemon juice
1–2 tablespoons water

Filling
300 g smoked cod fillet
3 eggs, lightly beaten
1/2 cup cream
1/2 cup grated cheddar cheese
1 tablespoon chopped fresh dill

➤ PREHEAT OVEN to hot 210°C (415°F/Gas Mark 6–7).

1 Place flour and butter in food processor. Process for 15 seconds until mixture is fine and crumbly. Add egg, juice and almost all the water, process for 30 seconds until mixture just comes together. Turn dough onto lightly floured surface. Press together gently until smooth. Cover with plastic wrap and leave in the refrigerator for about 20 minutes.

2 Roll pastry between two sheets of plastic wrap, large enough to cover base and sides of 22 cm fluted flan tin. Cut a sheet of greaseproof paper large enough to cover pastry-lined tin. Spread a layer of dried beans or rice evenly over paper. Bake 10 minutes. Remove from oven, discard paper and beans. Return pastry to oven for a further 5 minutes or until lightly golden. Remove from oven and allow pastry to cool slightly. Reduce oven temperature to moderate 180°C.

3 To make Filling: Flake cod into small pieces, using a fork. Combine eggs, cream, cheese and dill in bowl. Add cod. Mix well. Spoon mixture into pie shell. Bake for 40 minutes or until set. Eat hot or cold served with wedges of lemon or lime and a green salad.

COOK'S FILE

Storage time: Should be eaten the day it is made.

Hint: Smoked cod is available in delicatessens and fish shops.

Variation: Smoked oysters or mussels may be used in this recipe.

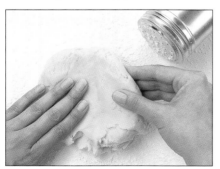

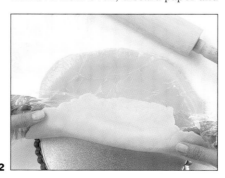

TUNA AND WHITE BEAN CASSEROLE

Preparation time: 40 minutes +
overnight soaking
Total cooking time: 3 hours
Serves 6

2 cups dried cannellini beans
1/4 cup olive oil
2 medium red onions, chopped
2 cloves garlic, crushed
1 teaspoon ground coriander
1 teaspoon finely grated lemon
  rind
2 teaspoons finely chopped
  thyme
2 cups good quality white wine
2 cups fish stock
475 g can tuna, drained
1 bunch basil, leaves only
4 large ripe tomatoes, cut in
  1 cm slices

Topping
1/2 cup fresh breadcrumbs
1 clove garlic, crushed
1/2 cup finely chopped fresh
  parsley
30 g butter, melted

➤ SOAK BEANS in water overnight.
Drain.
1 Heat oil in large heavy-based pan.
Add onions, garlic, coriander, rind and
thyme. Cook over medium heat 10–15
minutes or until well softened. Add
beans, cook for further 10 minutes.
2 Add wine and stock. Cook, covered,
over low heat 2 hours or until beans
are tender (but not mashed).
3 Preheat oven to hot 210°C (415°F/
Gas Mark 6–7). Transfer mixture to
large ovenproof casserole dish. Top
with tuna. Sprinkle over basil leaves.
Lay tomato slices over basil.
4 To make Topping: Combine
breadcrumbs, garlic and parsley in

small bowl. Sprinkle mixture over
tomato. Drizzle with butter, bake
30 minutes or until top is golden.
Serve with crusty bread.

COOK'S FILE

Storage time: This dish can be
made a day in advance.
Variation: Canned salmon may be
used in this recipe if you prefer but
tuna is traditional with beans. May
be served with a crisp, green salad.

MARINARA CASSEROLE

Preparation time: 25 minutes
Total cooking time: 1 hour
Serves 6–8

5 large tomatoes
2 tablespoons olive oil
1 large onion, thinly sliced
4 cloves garlic, crushed
2 tablespoons tomato paste
1 teaspoon sugar
1 teaspoon salt
1/2 teaspoon sweet paprika
1 cup good quality red wine
500 g green king prawns
500 g ling or perch fillets

500 g baby octopus
2 cups water
3 cups shell pasta
1/4 cup chopped parsley
1 tablespoon chopped oregano
1 tablespoon chopped chives
1 tablespoon finely grated
   lemon rind

➤ PREHEAT OVEN to hot 210°C
(415°F/Gas Mark 6–7).
1 Peel tomatoes, remove seeds and
cut into 2 cm pieces. Heat oil in large
pan. Add onion, cook 5 minutes until
soft. Stir in garlic, tomatoes, tomato
paste, sugar, salt, paprika and wine.
Cover, simmer for 15 minutes.
2 Peel prawns leaving tails intact.
Cut the fish into 3 cm cubes; clean

octopus, cut each into 3 pieces. Heat
water in large shallow pan, simmer
fish and octopus for 2 minutes and
prawns for 1 minute. Remove with a
slotted spoon, set aside. Reserve liquid.
3 Transfer tomato mixture to a
10-cup capacity casserole dish, add
liquid and pasta; stir to combine.
Bake covered 25 minutes. Add fish,
octopus and prawns, cook 5 minutes.
Sprinkle over combined parsley,
oregano, chives and lemon rind.

COOK'S FILE

Storage time: Casserole is best
eaten the day it is made.
Hint: If dish does not have a lid,
cover loosely with greased aluminium
foil. Use fish stock instead of wine.

ITALIAN FISH ROLLS

Preparation time: 25 minutes
Total cooking time: 20 minutes
Serves 4–6

1 tablespoon capers, chopped
1/4 cup stuffed green olives,
   chopped
1/4 cup finely chopped fresh
   lemon thyme
1 large tomato, peeled, seeded
   and chopped

1/4 cup finely grated romano
   cheese
2 teaspoons finely grated lemon
   rind
1/4 teaspoon freshly ground
   black pepper
8 thin white fish fillets (850 g)
1 cup good quality white wine
2 tablespoons lemon juice
1/4 cup fresh lemon thyme leaves
2 bay leaves

➤ PREHEAT OVEN to warm 160°C
(315°F/Gas Mark 2–3).

1 Combine capers, olives, thyme,
tomato, cheese, lemon rind and black
pepper in small bowl; mix well.
2 Place fillets skin-side down onto a
flat surface. Spread mixture evenly
onto each fillet. Roll each fillet tightly,
secure with a toothpick or skewer.
Place in single layer in casserole dish.
3 Pour over combined wine, juice,
thyme and bay leaves. Cover, bake
for 20 minutes or until fish is cooked.

COOK'S FILE

Storage time: Serve immediately.

Marinara Casserole (top)
and Italian Fish Rolls.

GREEK STYLE CALAMARI

Preparation time: 30 minutes
Total cooking time: 35 minutes
Serves 4–6

1 kg medium tubes calamari

Stuffing
1 tablespoon olive oil
2 spring onions, chopped
1 1/2 cups cooked rice
1/3 cup pine nuts
1/2 cup currants
**2 tablespoons chopped fresh
    parsley**
**2 teaspoons finely grated lemon
    rind**
1 egg, lightly beaten

Sauce
1 tablespoon olive oil
1 onion, finely chopped
1 clove garlic, crushed
**4 large ripe tomatoes, peeled
    and chopped**
1/4 cup good quality red wine
**1 tablespoon chopped fresh
    oregano**

➤ PREHEAT OVEN to warm 160°C (315°F/Gas Mark 2–3). Wash and dry calamari tubes.

1 Combine oil, onions, rice, pine nuts, currants, parsley and lemon rind in bowl. Mix well. Add enough egg to moisten all ingredients.

2 Three-quarters fill each tube. Secure end with toothpick or skewer. Place in single layer in casserole dish.

3 To make Sauce: Heat oil in medium pan; add onion and garlic and cook over low heat 2 minutes or until onion is soft. Add tomatoes, red wine and oregano. Cover and cook over low heat for 10 minutes. Pour sauce over calamari; cover and bake for 20 minutes or until calamari is tender. Remove toothpicks before cutting into thick slices for serving. Spoon sauce over just before serving.

COOK'S FILE

Storage time: Calamari is best eaten on day of preparation. Sauce can be made day before required.

Hint: To ensure a tender dish you must either cook squid very quickly over high heat or very slowly over low heat. Otherwise it will be tough.

1

2

3

INDEX

Ruler markings (left margin, top to bottom): 1 cm, 2 cm, 3 cm, 4 cm, 5 cm, 6 cm, 7 cm, 8 cm, 9 cm, 10 cm, 11 cm, 12 cm, 13 cm, 14 cm, 15 cm, 16 cm, 17 cm, 18 cm, 19 cm, 20 cm, 21 cm, 22 cm, 23 cm, 24 cm, 25 cm

USEFUL INFORMATION

All our recipes are tested in the Australian Family Circle® Test Kitchen. Standard metric measuring cups and spoons approved by Standard Australia are used in the development of our recipes. All cup and spoon measurements are level. We have used 60 g (Grade 3) eggs in all recipes. Sizes of cans vary from manufacturer to manufacturer and between countries—use the can size closest to the one suggested in the recipe.

Conversion Guide

1 cup	= 250 ml (8 fl oz)
1 teaspoon	= 5 ml
1 Australian tablespoon	= 20 ml (4 teaspoons)
1 UK/US tablespoon	= 15 ml (3 teaspoons)

NOTE: We have used 20 ml tablespoon measures. If you are using a 15 ml tablespoon, for most recipes the difference will not be noticeable. However, for recipes using baking powder, gelatine, bicarbonate of soda, small amounts of four and cornflour, add an extra teaspoon for each tablespoon specified.

Dry Measures	Liquid Measures	Linear Measure
30 g = 1 oz	30 ml = 1 fl oz	6 mm = 1/2 inch
250 g = 8 oz	125 ml = 4 fl oz	1 cm = 1/2 inch
500 g = 1 lb	250 ml = 8 fl oz	2.5 cm = 1 inch

Cup Conversions

1 cup plain flour	= 125 g (4 oz)
1 cup self-raising flour	= 125 g (4 oz)
1 cup grated Parmesan cheese	= 100 g ($3\frac{1}{4}$ oz)
1 cup fresh breadcrumbs	= 80 g ($2\frac{3}{4}$ oz)
1 cup peas	= 155 g (5 oz)
1 cup chopped parsley	= 60 g (2 oz)
1 cup tomato paste	= 250 g (8 oz)
1 cup sultanas	= 125 g (4 oz)
1 cup pine nuts	= 155 g (5 oz)

Oven Temperatures

Cooking times may vary slightly depending on the type of oven you are using. Before you preheat the oven, we suggest that you refer to the manufacturer's instructions to ensure proper temperature control.

	°C	°F	Gas Mark
Very Slow	120	250	1/2
Slow	150	300	2
Warm	170	325	3
Moderate	180	350	4
Mod. hot	190	375	5
Mod. hot	200	400	6
Hot	220	425	7
Very hot	230	450	8

NOTE: For fan-forced ovens check your appliance manual, but as a general rule, set oven temperature to 20°C lower than the temperature indicated in the recipe.

International Glossary

capsicum	red or green pepper
eggplant	aubergine
green prawns	raw prawns
plain flour	all-purpose flour
prawns	shrimp
silverbeet	swiss chard
zucchini	courgette

First published 1994 by Murdoch Books Pty Limited. Reprinted 1996, 1997, 1998, 1999, 2003. This edition published in 2004 for Index Books Ltd: Henson Way, Kettering, NN16 8PX, UK.
Printed by 1010 Printing Ltd. in China.

Editorial Director: Diana Hill. **Food Editors:** Kerrie Ray, Tracy Rutherford. **Editor:** Anna Sanders. **Designer:** Marylouise Brammer, Annette Fitzgerald, Jackie Richards. **Recipe Development:** Tracy Rutherford, Tracey Port, Kerrie Carr, Ken Gomes, Jody Vassallo, Beverley Sutherland Smith. **Food Stylist:** Mary Harris. **Photographers:** Jon Bader, Luis Martin, Andrew Furlong and Reg Morrison (Steps) **Food Preparation:** Melanie McDermott. **CEO:** Juliet Rogers. **Publisher:** Kay Scarlett